# The Singles Prayer Book: 50 Biblical Declarations to Become and Attract the Right Spouse

# TABLE OF *Contents*

*Introduction: The Singles Prayer Book* — 5

**Section 1 | Preparing your heart and Spirit** — 9

*Chapter 1: Discernment in Choosing a Spouse* — 10

*Chapter 2: Wisdom in Choosing a Spouse* — 15

*Chapter 3: Patience in God's Timing* — 20

*Chapter 4: The End Will Be Better Than the Beginning* — 25

*Chapter 5: Visibility for Marriage Opportunities* — 30

*Chapter 6: Declarations for Sexual Purity* — 35

*Chapter 7: Declarations for Boundaries with In-Laws* — 40

*Chapter 8: Declarations for the Little Foxes* — 45

*Chapter 9: Declarations Against Distraction* — 50

*Chapter 10: Declarations for Guarding the Heart* — 55

**Section 2 | Spiritual Warfare and Sexual Purity** — 60

*Chapter 11: Declarations for Becoming a Virtuous Woman* — 61

*Chapter 12: Declarations for Becoming a Valorous Husband* — 66

*Chapter 13: Declarations for Financial Provision and Generational Wealth* — 71

*Chapter 14: Declarations to Satan-Proof Your Marriage* — 76

*Chapter 15: Declarations for Engagement Warfare* — 81

*Chapter 16: Declarations for the Wedding Day* — 86

*Chapter 17: Declarations for Groomsmen to Say Over the Groom* — 91

Chapter 18: Declarations for Bridesmaids to Say Over the Bride　96

Chapter 19: Declarations for Mothers to Say Over Their Sons on the Wedding Day　101

Chapter 20: Declarations for Mothers to Say Over Their Daughters on the Wedding Day　106

**Section 3 | Becoming the Right Partner**　111

Chapter 21: Declarations for Fathers to Say Over Their Sons on the Wedding Day　112

Chapter 22: Declarations for Fathers to Say Over Their Daughters on the Wedding Day　117

Chapter 23: Declarations Over Your Son for Their Spouse　122

Chapter 24: Declarations Over Your Daughter for Their Spouse　127

Chapter 25: Declarations That Break Marital Delay　132

Chapter 26: Declarations to Find a Godly Man　137

**Section 4 | Preparing for Marriage**　142

Chapter 27: Declarations to Find a Godly Woman　143

Chapter 28: Declarations to Break Cycles of Distrust　148

Chapter 29: Declarations to Break Emotional Baggage　153

Chapter 30: Declarations to Reverse Curses Spoken Over You　158

Chapter 31: Declarations for Grace to Be Single　163

Chapter 32: Declarations and Repentance for Sexual Impurity　169

Chapter 33: Declarations Against Pornography and Lust for Him　174

Chapter 34: Declarations Against Pornography and Lust for Her　179

Chapter 35: Spiritual Warfare Declarations for Singles　184

**Section 5 | Protecting Marriage and Family**     *189*

*Chapter 36: Declarations for Wisdom to Build a Home*     *190*

*Chapter 37: Declarations for Family Disputes Against Your Spouse*     *195*

*Chapter 38: Declarations to Break Ungodly Soul Ties with a Controlling Father*     *200*

*Chapter 39: Declarations to Break Ungodly Soul Ties with a Controlling Mother*     *205*

*Chapter 40: Declarations Over a Child Born Through Sexual Sin*     *210*

*Chapter 41: Declarations for Feelings of Shame, Fear, and Guilt*     *215*

*Chapter 42: Declarations to War Against Satan's Wicked Thoughts*     *220*

*Chapter 43: Declarations Against Loneliness*     *225*

**Section 6 | Overcoming Spiritual Manipulation**     *229*

*Chapter 44: Declarations to Break the Spirit of Rejection*     *230*

*Chapter 45: Declarations Against Wet Dreams*     *235*

*Chapter 46: Declarations Against Breakup and Heartbreak*     *240*

*Chapter 47: Declarations Against Anxiety for the Future*     *245*

**Section 7 | Establishing Generational Blessings**     *249*

*Chapter 48: Declarations Against Prophetic Manipulation*     *250*

*Chapter 49: Declarations Against Love Spells and Incantations*     *255*

*Chapter 50: Declarations Against Fear of Making the Wrong Choice*     *259*

# INTRODUCTION

## "Wisdom Builds the House, Faith Opens the Door"

One day in Luke 11:1, one of Jesus disciples asked Him to teach them how to pray. Jesus never dismissed this, He instead prescribed for them a protocol and script so that prayers do not go amiss. Today I recognize the lack of teaching on prayer, so often what we call prayer has become a wishlist to written to God like a Christmas list to the North Pole. The Bible says that all God's promises through Christ are 'Yes and Amen' (2 Corinthians 1:20), simply put, God can never tell Himself 'No!' So if you and I can just learn to put His words in our mouths and voice them back to Him, then we too will experience a God who can never tell us 'No!' This book is designed to teach you how you ought to pray. It provides you with words to say but it doesn't provide you with the heart to say it, that must come from you!

> *For with the heart one believes unto righteousness,*
> *and with the mouth confession is made unto salvation.*
> *Romans 10:10 (NKJV)*

Marriage is one of life's greatest gifts—a sacred covenant designed by God, not just to fulfill companionship but to reflect His divine relationship with the church. Yet today, prayer for a spouse is often treated casually, as though marriage were merely a checklist item or a convenience. We pray with half-hearted faith, asking God for what we want while ignoring the wisdom required to sustain what we are asking for. This book is a clarion call to a deeper understanding: **prayer for a spouse is both a spiritual declaration and a practical preparation.**

The Bible offers us powerful blueprints of how heaven orchestrates godly unions. When the angel spoke to Joseph, it wasn't just to inform him of Mary's divine pregnancy; it was to reassure him not to fear stepping into his God-given role as her husband. Abraham prayed for his servant to find a wife for Isaac, and that servant, filled with faith and divine guidance, prayed to the Lord for a sign—a woman who would offer him water and care for his camels. This wasn't mere coincidence; it was the hand of God in response to intentional, faith-filled prayers. These examples remind us that marriage, when divinely orchestrated, is a covenant, not a coincidence.

But what happens when the covenant is broken? Divorce, rooted in idolatry, domestic violence, or abandonment, represents the crushing defeat of God's original design. Scripture, while protective of the sanctity of marriage, does not ignore the realities of human failure. Jesus Himself acknowledged that sexual sin and abandonment violate the sacred bond, and Paul, writing to the early church, explained that leadership required a new way of life: monogamy and devotion in a culture steeped in polygamy. Acts 17:30 reminds us of God's mercy: **"In the past, God overlooked such ignorance, but now He commands all people everywhere to repent."**

My prayer is that for those who have experienced divorce or ignorance regarding marriage, this book offers not condemnation, but clarity. If you lived with an uninformed view of marriage until now, know that God extends grace. However, understand this: marriage is final. It is not a contract to be broken, but a covenant sealed with blood, as designed by God through the act of sexual intimacy. This is not a light or temporary union; it is eternal in its significance.

This book is not for those seeking a quick fix or a surface repentance for sin. It is not for those cohabiting, fornicating, or treating God's covenant lightly. This book is for those who are ready to align their lives—spiritually, emotionally, and practically—for marriage. It is for those who understand that **wisdom builds the house** (Proverbs 24:3-4) and that **faith speaks those things that are not as though they were** (Romans 4:17). It is for those who are ready to fight for their destiny in prayer, declaration, and preparation.

Marriage is not simply about finding the right person; it's about becoming the right person. It requires spiritual fortitude, emotional maturity, and the wisdom to build a house that will stand against the storms of life. This is your year to be married. But it will not come through idleness or wishful thinking; it will come through alignment, intentionality, and uncompromising conviction.

In the pages ahead, you will find declarations to break cycles of delay, prayers to guard your heart, and wisdom to discern God's will for your future spouse. This is not a book for the fainthearted but for those who are ready to claim their place in God's design for love and covenant.

Are you ready to pray with power, align with purpose, and step into the marriage God has prepared for you? Then turn the page, because **your season of waiting is about to transform into a season of divine fulfilment.**

This is your year. Let's begin.

# SECTION 1

## PREPARING YOUR HEART AND SPIRIT

# CHAPTER 1

## Discernment in Choosing a Spouse

***Scripture Focus:***
*"You will also declare a thing, and it will be established for you; so light will shine on your ways."*
*Job 22:28 (NKJV)*

**Introduction:**
Discernment is a gift from the Lord that enables us to see beyond the natural and perceive the spiritual truth. It is a sacred weapon in the battle for a godly life and marriage. Discernment is not suspicion—where fear and doubt disguise themselves as wisdom—but a divine ability to judge rightly, guided by the Spirit of truth.

Today, many are led astray by counterfeit relationships, ensnared by appearances, and distracted by smooth words. This is where discernment, fueled by the Word of God and the leading of the Holy Spirit, becomes your greatest safeguard.

The enemy seeks to sow confusion, but the light of God will expose every deception. As you pray these declarations, you are sharpening your spirit, breaking the schemes of the enemy, and positioning yourself for divine alignment.

**20 Declarations for Discernment:**

1. Father, in the name of Jesus, I decree and declare that my steps are ordered by You, according to Your Word that says, 'The steps of a good man are ordered by the Lord, and He delights in his way' (Psalm 37:23). I align my heart with Your will and declare that every step I take brings me closer to Your ordained purpose for my life. I rebuke confusion and declare clarity in every decision concerning my future spouse.

2. Lord, I decree and declare in accordance with Proverbs 3:5-6 that I will trust in You with all my heart and lean not on my own understanding. In all my ways, I acknowledge You, and I declare that You are making my paths straight. Every crooked place in my journey is being made smooth by Your hand.

3. I declare, Lord, that I have the mind of Christ, as written in 1 Corinthians 2:16. I reject every thought of suspicion and paranoia that the enemy has planted to distort my perception. I will discern righteously, not through fear, but through the wisdom and peace of Your Spirit.

4. Holy Spirit, I decree and declare, as Jesus promised in John 16:13, that You are the Spirit of truth who guides me into all truth. Reveal the hidden things, expose every lie, and lead me into divine connections that align with Your will.

5. Father, I declare, according to 1 Samuel 16:7, that I will not judge by outward appearances, for You look at the heart. Give me eyes to see as You see and a heart that aligns with Your wisdom, so I will not be deceived by charm, wealth, or status.

6. In the name of Jesus, I rebuke every spirit of manipulation and deception assigned to distract me from Your purpose. According to Isaiah 54:17, no weapon formed against me shall prosper, and every tongue that rises against me in judgment, I condemn. I silence the voices of the enemy trying to confuse or mislead me.

7. Lord, I decree that Your peace, which surpasses all understanding, guards my heart and mind in Christ Jesus, as written in Philippians 4:7. I will not be driven by anxiety or desperation but by Your perfect peace in every decision.

8. I declare that I will not be unequally yoked, in accordance with 2 Corinthians 6:14. Every ungodly relationship is severed now in Jesus' name. Align me with someone who shares my faith, purpose, and covenant with You.

9. Heavenly Father, I declare that the light of Your Word, which is a lamp to my feet and a light to my path (Psalm 119:105), shines on every area of darkness. Illuminate every hidden intention, every hidden trap, and lead me into truth.

10. Father, I declare that I am surrounded by godly counsel, according to Proverbs 11:14. Place mentors, leaders, and wise advisors in my life who will help me discern rightly and avoid costly mistakes.

11. Lord, I decree that my spirit is trained to discern good and evil, as written in Hebrews 5:14. I declare that I will not confuse suspicion with discernment. Suspicion is rooted in fear, but discernment is born of faith and wisdom. I will operate in faith and not fear!

12. In the name of Jesus, I break every spirit of distraction assigned to divert me from God's best. I declare, as written in Isaiah 30:21, that I will hear a voice behind me saying, 'This is the way; walk in it,' whenever I turn to the right or left.

13. Father, I decree, in alignment with 2 Timothy 1:7, that I am not given a spirit of fear but of power, love, and a sound mind. I cast out every fearful thought that seeks to cloud my judgment and declare that I have clarity and boldness.

14. Lord, I declare that my desires are aligned with Your Word, as written in Psalm 37:4: 'Delight yourself in the Lord, and He will give you the desires of your heart.' I delight in You and trust that my desires are purified by Your Spirit.

15. I decree that every counterfeit relationship is exposed and destroyed. According to 2 Timothy 3:5, I will have nothing to do with those who have a form of godliness but deny its power. I declare that my spirit recognizes the truth and rejects the false.

16. Father, I declare in Jesus' name that Your favor surrounds me like a shield, as written in Psalm 5:12. Let Your favor guide me to the right person and protect me from every wrong connection.

17. I decree and declare, in alignment with Ecclesiastes 3:11, that You make everything beautiful in its time. I reject impatience, and I trust Your timing completely.

18. I declare, Lord, that I will follow Your voice, as written in John 10:27: 'My sheep listen to my voice; I know them, and they follow me.' I will not be swayed by strangers, distractions, or emotional impulses.

19. In the name of Jesus, I declare that I am free from every generational curse or pattern that has hindered godly marriages in my family. According to Galatians 3:13, Christ has redeemed me from the curse of the law. I walk in freedom and victory.

20. Father, I declare that Your Word establishes my steps, and I am firmly rooted in Your truth. As Job 22:28 says, I declare Your promises, and they are established in my life. I walk in the light of Your ways and trust You fully for my future.

**Closing Prayer:**
Father, I thank You for the gift of discernment. I pray that these declarations will establish light and clarity in every area of my life. Teach me to wait on You, to trust Your timing, and to seek Your wisdom above all else. May Your Spirit guide me into truth, exposing every scheme of the enemy and leading me into the covenant relationship You have ordained for me. In Jesus' name, Amen.

# CHAPTER 2

# Wisdom in Choosing a Spouse

***Scripture Focus:***
*"Through wisdom a house is built, and by understanding it is established; by knowledge the rooms are filled with all precious and pleasant riches."*
*Proverbs 24:3-4 (NKJV)*

**Introduction:**
Wisdom is the foundation of any lasting marriage. While love may light the flame, it is wisdom that sustains the fire. Too often, we make choices based on fleeting emotions or external appearances, forgetting that the wisdom of God builds what feelings alone cannot. Wisdom in choosing a spouse is not only about recognizing the right person but about preparing yourself to build a home that honors God.

Wisdom is active, intentional, and grounded in truth. It is the ability to see things from God's perspective and act accordingly. This chapter will guide you through declarations that invite God's wisdom into your decision-making, your relationships, and your vision for marriage.

As Proverbs 24:3-4 reminds us, wisdom builds the house, understanding establishes it, and knowledge fills it with treasures. These declarations will empower you to make decisions that lead to a marriage designed to glorify God and stand the test of time.

**20 Declarations for Wisdom in Choosing a Spouse**

1. Father, in the name of Jesus, I decree and declare that I am filled with godly wisdom, for Your Word says, 'If any of you lacks wisdom, let him ask of God, who gives to all liberally and without reproach, and it will be given to him' (James 1:5). I ask You now for wisdom in choosing a spouse, and I receive it in abundance.

2. Lord, I declare that I will build my future home on the foundation of wisdom, understanding, and knowledge, as written in Proverbs 24:3-4. Teach me to make decisions that are rooted in Your truth and guided by Your Spirit.

3. I decree that I am led by the Spirit of wisdom and revelation in the knowledge of You, as written in Ephesians 1:17. I will not be blinded by emotions or appearances but will seek Your insight in every decision.

4. Father, I declare that I will fear the Lord, for Your Word says, 'The fear of the Lord is the beginning of wisdom, and the knowledge of the Holy One is understanding' (Proverbs 9:10). I submit my choices to You, knowing that wisdom begins with reverence for You.

5. In the name of Jesus, I declare that I will discern the difference between worldly wisdom and godly wisdom. Your Word says, 'The wisdom of this world is foolishness with God' (1 Corinthians 3:19). I reject worldly counsel and embrace the wisdom that comes from above.

6. Lord, I decree that my heart will not be deceived by charm or outward beauty, for Your Word warns, 'Charm is deceitful and beauty is passing, but a woman who fears the Lord, she shall be praised' (Proverbs 31:30). I will seek character over charisma.

7. I declare that I will not make hasty decisions in relationships, for Your Word says, 'The plans of the diligent lead surely to plenty, but those of everyone who is hasty, surely to poverty' (Proverbs 21:5). I will move with wisdom and patience.

8. Father, I decree that I will test every spirit and align my relationships with Your Word, for You said, 'Beloved, do not believe every spirit, but test the spirits to see whether they are from God' (1 John 4:1). I will not be led astray by counterfeit relationships.

9. In the name of Jesus, I declare that I will seek wise counsel, for 'Where there is no counsel, the people fall; but in the multitude of counselors, there is safety' (Proverbs 11:14). Surround me with godly voices that speak truth and wisdom into my life.

10. Lord, I declare that my future spouse will be a partner who walks in wisdom and aligns with Your purpose for my life, for Your Word says, 'Can two walk together unless they are agreed?' (Amos 3:3). I will not compromise on spiritual alignment.

11. Father, I declare that I will prioritize Your kingdom in every decision, for Jesus said, 'Seek first the kingdom of God and His righteousness, and all these things shall be added to you' (Matthew 6:33). I trust that as I seek You, everything else will fall into place.

12. I decree that I will listen to Your voice and not follow the voice of a stranger, as written in John 10:27. I will not be confused or misled but will follow Your guidance in choosing a spouse.

13. Lord, I declare that I will recognize the fruits of the Spirit in my future spouse, for Your Word says, 'By their fruits you will know them' (Matthew 7:16). I will not ignore red flags or signs of ungodliness.

14. In the name of Jesus, I declare that I will not be conformed to the patterns of this world but transformed by the renewing of my mind, as written in Romans 12:2. I will choose a spouse with a renewed mind and a heart aligned with You.

15. Father, I decree that I will walk in peace, for Your Word says, 'Let the peace of God rule in your hearts' (Colossians 3:15). I will not proceed in any relationship that lacks Your peace.

16. Lord, I declare that my future marriage will reflect Your wisdom, for Your Word says, 'A wise woman builds her house, but the foolish pulls it down with her hands' (Proverbs 14:1). Teach me to build wisely.

17. I decree that my decisions are led by love and not fear, for Your Word says, 'There is no fear in love, but perfect love casts out

fear' (1 John 4:18). I will not be motivated by desperation or insecurity.

18. Father, I declare that I will meditate on Your Word day and night, as written in Joshua 1:8, and that Your wisdom will direct my path in every area of my life, including marriage.

19. In the name of Jesus, I declare that I will guard my heart with all diligence, for Your Word says, 'Above all else, guard your heart, for everything you do flows from it' (Proverbs 4:23). I will not allow my emotions to lead me astray.

20. Lord, I decree and declare that I will walk in the light of Your wisdom and trust in Your perfect timing. Your Word says, 'He has made everything beautiful in its time' (Ecclesiastes 3:11). I trust that my marriage will be established in beauty and order, according to Your plan.

**Closing Prayer:**
Heavenly Father, I thank You for the gift of wisdom. I pray that these declarations will take root in my heart and bear fruit in every decision I make. Help me to walk in Your truth, guided by Your Spirit, and to make choices that align with Your will. Let my future marriage be a reflection of Your wisdom and glory. In Jesus' name, Amen.

# CHAPTER 3

# Patience in God's Timing

**Scripture Focus:**
*"Wait on the Lord; be of good courage, and
He shall strengthen your heart; wait, I say, on the Lord!"
Psalm 27:14 (NKJV)*

**Introduction:**

Patience is not passivity; it is active trust in God's perfect timing. In a world that values instant gratification, waiting on the Lord feels like an impossible task. But patience, when coupled with faith, is a powerful expression of trust in God's sovereignty. It says, "Lord, I believe Your timing is better than mine, and I surrender my plans to You."

Impatience can lead to costly mistakes, but those who wait on the Lord renew their strength (Isaiah 40:31). They are not wearied by the delays of life but empowered by His promises. In this chapter, you will declare the promises of patience and rebuke the spirit of haste, anxiety, and desperation. These declarations will build resilience, peace, and unwavering confidence in God's perfect plan for your life.

# 20 Declarations for Patience in God's Timing

1. Father, in the name of Jesus, I decree and declare that I will wait on You with confidence, for Your Word says, 'Wait on the Lord; be of good courage, and He shall strengthen your heart; wait, I say, on the Lord!' (Psalm 27:14). I trust that Your timing is perfect and that You are strengthening my heart as I wait.

2. Lord, I declare that I am not anxious about my future, for Your Word says, 'Be anxious for nothing, but in everything by prayer and supplication, with thanksgiving, let your requests be made known to God; and the peace of God, which surpasses all understanding, will guard your hearts and minds through Christ Jesus' (Philippians 4:6-7). Your peace guards my heart and mind as I trust in You.

3. I decree that I will not grow weary in doing good, for Your Word says, 'And let us not grow weary while doing good, for in due season we shall reap if we do not lose heart' (Galatians 6:9). I declare that my due season is coming, and I will reap a harvest of blessings in Your time.

4. Father, I declare that I am still and know that You are God, as written in Psalm 46:10. I silence every voice of fear, doubt, and impatience, and I rest in the assurance that You are in control of my life.

5. Lord, I rebuke the spirit of haste and declare that I am aligned with Your divine calendar. Your Word says, 'To everything there is a season, a time for every purpose under heaven' (Ecclesiastes 3:1). I declare that I will not move ahead of Your plan but will trust

Your perfect timing.

6. I decree that I am filled with the fruit of patience, for Your Word says, 'But the fruit of the Spirit is love, joy, peace, long-suffering, kindness, goodness, faithfulness, gentleness, self-control' (Galatians 5:22-23). Patience flows abundantly in my life as I walk in Your Spirit.

7. Father, I declare that I will not compare my journey to others, for Your Word says, 'Let us run with endurance the race that is set before us' (Hebrews 12:1). I am focused on the unique race You have marked out for me.

8. Lord, I decree that my waiting is not in vain, for Your Word says, 'The Lord is good to those who wait for Him, to the soul who seeks Him' (Lamentations 3:25). I declare that Your goodness is manifesting in my life as I wait on You.

9. I declare that I will not settle for less than Your best, for Your Word says, 'Every good gift and every perfect gift is from above, and comes down from the Father of lights' (James 1:17). I trust that You are preparing a perfect gift in the form of a godly spouse.

10. In the name of Jesus, I declare that I am patient in affliction and faithful in prayer, for Your Word says, 'Be joyful in hope, patient in affliction, faithful in prayer' (Romans 12:12). My joy is unshaken because I know that Your promises are sure.

11. Father, I rebuke every spirit of discouragement and declare that I am strengthened by Your Word, which says, 'But those who

wait on the Lord shall renew their strength; they shall mount up with wings like eagles, they shall run and not be weary, they shall walk and not faint' (Isaiah 40:31). I rise with renewed strength as I wait on You.

12. Lord, I decree that I am content in every season, for Your Word says, 'Now godliness with contentment is great gain' (1 Timothy 6:6). I declare that my heart is satisfied in You, and I will not strive or complain.

13. I declare that I trust Your ability to redeem time, for Your Word says, 'I will restore to you the years that the swarming locust has eaten' (Joel 2:25). Every delay and loss in my life is being restored in Your perfect plan.

14. In the name of Jesus, I declare that I am free from the pressure of societal expectations. Your Word says, 'For do I now persuade men, or God? Or do I seek to please men? For if I still pleased men, I would not be a bondservant of Christ' (Galatians 1:10). I live to please You alone, Lord.

15. Father, I declare that my hope is alive and active, for Your Word says, 'Hope does not disappoint, because the love of God has been poured out in our hearts by the Holy Spirit who was given to us' (Romans 5:5). My hope in You is steadfast and unwavering.

16. Lord, I decree that I am rooted and grounded in Your love, for Your Word says, 'May your roots go down deep into the soil of God's marvelous love' (Ephesians 3:17, NLT). I am nourished and secure in Your love, and I will not be moved by impatience.

17. I declare that I am anxious for nothing, as Philippians 4:6-7 commands, but instead, I bring my requests to You with thanksgiving, trusting that Your peace will guard my heart and mind.

18. Father, I declare that my future spouse is also waiting on You, and You are preparing them in this season. Your Word says, 'The Lord will perfect that which concerns me' (Psalm 138:8). I trust that You are working all things together for our good.

19. In the name of Jesus, I decree that my faith is unwavering, for Your Word says, 'Let us hold fast the confession of our hope without wavering, for He who promised is faithful' (Hebrews 10:23). I stand firm on Your promises.

20. Lord, I declare that I will wait in expectation and not in despair, for Your Word says, 'I wait for the Lord, my soul waits, and in His word I do hope' (Psalm 130:5). My hope is rooted in Your faithfulness, and I trust You completely.

**Closing Prayer:**
Father, I thank You for the gift of patience. As I declare these words, I receive Your peace, strength, and assurance. Help me to wait with joy, knowing that You are working all things
together for my good. Teach me to trust in Your timing and to honor You in this season. I surrender my desires to You, knowing that You will fulfill them in Your perfect way. In Jesus' name, Amen.

# CHAPTER 4

# The End Will Be Better Than the Beginning

***Scripture Focus:***
*"Better is the end of a thing than its beginning, and the patient in spirit is better than the proud in spirit."*
*Ecclesiastes 7:8 (ESV)*

**Introduction:**
The journey toward a godly marriage may be filled with trials, delays, and setbacks, but God's promise is this: **the end will be better than the beginning.** No matter how broken your past, how delayed your dreams, or how painful your journey, God is the ultimate Restorer. He specializes in transforming ashes into beauty and turning mourning into joy.

It is easy to feel discouraged by how things began—mistakes made, relationships lost, or time seemingly wasted. But Ecclesiastes 7:8 reminds us that the end is worth waiting for. In this chapter, you will declare God's promises for restoration, redemption, and a future that far exceeds your expectations. These declarations will lift your faith, rebuke discouragement and position you to walk boldly into a better ending—God's divine plan for your life.

**20 Declarations for a Better Ending**

1. Father, in the name of Jesus, I decree and declare that the latter days of my life will be far greater than the former, for Your Word says, 'Better is the end of a thing than its beginning, and the patient in spirit is better than the proud in spirit' (Ecclesiastes 7:8). I declare that my story is not over, and You are writing a glorious ending.

2. Lord, I declare that You are a God of restoration, for Your Word says, 'I will restore to you the years that the swarming locust has eaten' (Joel 2:25). I decree that every delay, loss, and disappointment in my life is being redeemed for Your glory.

3. I decree that my future is filled with hope and peace, as Your Word declares in Jeremiah 29:11: 'For I know the plans I have for you, declares the Lord, plans for welfare and not for evil, to give you a future and a hope.' I trust in Your perfect plans for my life.

4. Father, I declare that my path is shining brighter and brighter, for Your Word says, 'The path of the righteous is like the light of dawn, which shines brighter and brighter until full day' (Proverbs 4:18). My tomorrow is better than my today.

5. Lord, I decree that You are turning every sorrow into joy, for Your Word says, 'You have turned for me my mourning into dancing; You have loosed my sackcloth and clothed me with gladness' (Psalm 30:11). I declare that joy is my portion.

6. In the name of Jesus, I rebuke every voice of discouragement and despair. Your Word says, 'Why are you cast down, O my soul, and why are you in turmoil within me? Hope in God; for I shall again praise Him, my salvation and my God' (Psalm 42:11). I choose hope and praise over doubt and fear.

7. Father, I declare that You are doing a new thing in my life, as written in Isaiah 43:19: 'Behold, I am doing a new thing; now it springs forth, do you not perceive it? I will make a way in the wilderness and rivers in the desert.' My past will not define my future.

8. Lord, I decree that You are able to do exceedingly abundantly above all I could ask or think, as written in Ephesians 3:20. I declare that my future marriage will exceed every hope and expectation.

9. In the name of Jesus, I declare that my ending will be marked by peace and blessing, for Your Word says, 'Mark the blameless man, and observe the upright; for the future of that man is peace' (Psalm 37:37). I declare that peace is my inheritance.

10. Father, I decree that You crown my year with goodness, as written in Psalm 65:11: 'You crown the year with Your goodness, and Your paths drip with abundance.' I declare that abundance and favor follow me into this season.

11. Lord, I declare that my faith will not fail, for Your Word says, 'And I am sure of this, that He who began a good work in you will bring it to completion at the day of Jesus Christ' (Philippians 1:6). You will finish what You started in me.

12. I declare that my testimony will bring glory to God, for Your Word says, 'And they overcame him by the blood of the Lamb and by the word of their testimony' (Revelation 12:11). My future marriage will testify of Your goodness and faithfulness.

13. Father, I decree that every setback is being turned into a setup for Your glory. Your Word says, 'And we know that all things work together for good to those who love God, to those who are the called according to His purpose' (Romans 8:28). My story is working for my good.

14. Lord, I rebuke every lie of the enemy that says my best days are behind me. Your Word says, 'The glory of this latter temple shall be greater than the former' (Haggai 2:9). My latter days will be glorious.

15. I decree that I will walk boldly into my future, for Your Word says, 'Forget the former things; do not dwell on the past' (Isaiah 43:18). I release the past and embrace the new things You are doing.

16. Father, I declare that every tear I've cried is being redeemed, for Your Word says, 'Those who sow in tears shall reap in joy' (Psalm 126:5). I declare that joy is my portion.

17. Lord, I decree that my heart will not grow bitter, for Your Word says, 'Pursue peace with all people, and holiness, without which no one will see the Lord' (Hebrews 12:14). I choose peace and holiness over bitterness and regret.

18. I declare that I will run my race with endurance, for Your Word says, 'Let us run with endurance the race that is set before us, looking unto Jesus, the author and finisher of our faith' (Hebrews 12:1-2). My eyes are fixed on You, Lord.

19. Father, I declare that You are my portion and my strength. Your Word says, 'My flesh and my heart may fail, but God is the strength of my heart and my portion forever' (Psalm 73:26). I lean on You and not my own strength.

20. Lord, I decree and declare that the ending of this season will be marked by joy, fulfillment, and purpose, for Your Word says, 'Weeping may endure for a night, but joy comes in the morning' (Psalm 30:5). My morning is here, and joy is my inheritance.

**Closing Prayer:**
Father, I thank You for the promise that the end of a thing is better than its beginning. I trust that You are working all things together for my good and that You are writing a story far greater than I could imagine. I surrender my past, my present, and my future to You, knowing that Your plans for me are perfect. Let my life and my future marriage bring You glory. In Jesus' name, Amen.

# CHAPTER 5

# Visibility for Marriage Opportunities

***Scripture Focus:***
*"You are the light of the world.*
*A city that is set on a hill cannot be hidden."*
*Matthew 5:14 (NKJV)*

**Introduction:**
Visibility is not about seeking attention; it is about alignment with God's purpose so that you are seen by the right person at the right time. When you walk in God's light, He positions you in places where His plans for your life can unfold. Many singles feel invisible, overlooked, or hidden, but God has a divine time and stage for you.

Just as Ruth was seen by Boaz while faithfully working in the field, God will ensure that you are noticed as you walk in His will. These declarations are designed to break every spirit of obscurity, isolation, and delay. As Matthew 5:14 declares, you are a city on a hill—you cannot be hidden when you shine in His purpose. Declare these truths over your life, and step into the visibility God has ordained for you.

## 20 Declarations for Visibility

1. Father, in the name of Jesus, I decree and declare that I am a light set on a hill, as Your Word says in Matthew 5:14. I cannot be hidden because Your light shines through me, drawing the right people into my life at the appointed time.

2. Lord, I declare that my life is aligned with Your purpose, and as I walk in obedience, I am positioned for divine connections. Your Word says, 'The steps of a good man are ordered by the Lord, and He delights in his way' (Psalm 37:23). I trust that You are ordering my steps.

3. I decree that every veil of obscurity is removed from my life. Your Word says, 'Arise, shine; for your light has come! And the glory of the Lord is risen upon you' (Isaiah 60:1). I rise into visibility, shining with Your glory.

4. Father, I declare that just as Ruth found favor with Boaz in the field, I will find favor in the places where You have positioned me. Your Word says, 'For You, O Lord, will bless the righteous; with favor You will surround him as with a shield' (Psalm 5:12).

5. Lord, I decree that my gifts will make room for me, as written in Proverbs 18:16: 'A man's gift makes room for him, and brings him before great men.' I declare that the gifts You have placed in me will draw the right person into my life.

6. In the name of Jesus, I declare that every delay in my visibility is broken. Your Word says, 'He has made everything beautiful in its time' (Ecclesiastes 3:11). I trust that my time for visibility is now.

7. Father, I rebuke every spirit of rejection and insignificance. Your Word says, 'The stone which the builders rejected has become the chief cornerstone' (Psalm 118:22). I declare that I am accepted and valuable in Your plan.

8. Lord, I decree that I am noticed for the right reasons and by the right people. Your Word says, 'So let your light shine before men, that they may see your good works and glorify your Father in heaven' (Matthew 5:16). I walk in integrity and purpose, attracting godly connections.

9. Father, I declare that no plot of the enemy to hide me will prosper. Your Word says, 'No weapon formed against you shall prosper, and every tongue which rises against you in judgment you shall condemn' (Isaiah 54:17).

10. In the name of Jesus, I decree that divine opportunities will locate me. Your Word says, 'The eyes of the Lord run to and fro throughout the whole earth, to show Himself strong on behalf of those whose heart is loyal to Him' (2 Chronicles 16:9). I declare that Your eyes are upon me, Lord.

11. Lord, I declare that I am like a tree planted by the rivers of water, bearing fruit in its season, as written in Psalm 1:3. My life will be fruitful and evident to those You have called to walk with me.

12. Father, I decree that I will not be overlooked or bypassed. Your Word says, 'But the Lord said to Samuel, "Do not look at his appearance or at his physical stature, because I have refused him.

For the Lord does not see as man sees; for man looks at the outward appearance, but the Lord looks at the heart'" (1 Samuel 16:7). I declare that my heart is seen and valued.

13. Lord, I declare that I am prepared for the season of visibility. Your Word says, 'But sanctify the Lord God in your hearts, and always be ready to give a defense to everyone who asks you a reason for the hope that is in you' (1 Peter 3:15). I am ready to walk into my season.

14. In the name of Jesus, I decree that I am remembered and favored like Joseph in Pharaoh's court. Your Word says, 'And Pharaoh said to Joseph, "See, I have set you over all the land of Egypt"' (Genesis 41:41). I declare that I am remembered and elevated at the right time.

15. Father, I declare that my faithfulness is rewarded, just as David was found tending sheep when he was called to be king. Your Word says, 'If you are faithful in little things, you will be faithful in large ones' (Luke 16:10, NLT). I am faithful in my current season, and You are preparing me for greater things.

16. Lord, I decree that I will walk boldly into the doors You open, for Your Word says, 'I have set before you an open door, and no one can shut it' (Revelation 3:8). I declare that no fear or doubt will hold me back.

17. Father, I rebuke every lie of insignificance and declare that I am fearfully and wonderfully made, as written in Psalm 139:14. I embrace my identity and worth in You.

18. Lord, I decree that I will be seen as a blessing, for Your Word says, 'The blessing of the Lord makes one rich, and He adds no sorrow with it' (Proverbs 10:22). I will enrich the life of my future spouse by walking in Your blessing.

19. Father, I declare that divine connections are aligning even now, for Your Word says, 'The Lord has made everything for its purpose' (Proverbs 16:4). I trust that You are orchestrating my visibility for Your purpose.

20. Lord, I decree that I am stepping out of obscurity and into my appointed season. Your Word says, 'The Lord will open the heavens, the storehouse of His bounty, to send rain on your land in season and to bless all the work of your hands' (Deuteronomy 28:12). My season of visibility is here, and I walk in it boldly.

**Closing Prayer:**
Father, I thank You for the promise that I cannot be hidden when I walk in Your light. I declare that my season of visibility has come, and You are aligning me with divine opportunities and connections. Let every spirit of obscurity and delay be broken, and let Your favor rest upon me. I step into my season with confidence, knowing that You are guiding my every step. In Jesus' name, Amen.

# CHAPTER 6

# Declarations for Sexual Purity

***Scripture Focus:***
*"Blessed are the pure in heart, for they shall see God."*
*Matthew 5:8 (NKJV)*

**Introduction:**
Sexual purity is not just a physical discipline; it is a heart posture before God. In a world that normalizes immorality and treats abstinence as outdated, remaining pure is a bold declaration of faith and obedience to God's Word. Purity is about more than abstaining from sin; it is about protecting the covenant God has for your future marriage.

The enemy uses sexual temptation as a weapon to derail destinies, but through the power of the Holy Spirit, you can overcome every snare. Purity is possible. As Matthew 5:8 promises, the pure in heart will see God. These declarations will equip you to walk in holiness, resist temptation, and preserve your body, mind, and spirit for the covenant God has ordained for you.

## 20 Declarations for Sexual Purity

1. Father, in the name of Jesus, I decree and declare that my body is a temple of the Holy Spirit, as written in 1 Corinthians 6:19-20: 'Do you not know that your body is the temple of the Holy Spirit who is in you, whom you have from God, and you are not your own? For you were bought at a price; therefore glorify God in your body and in your spirit, which are God's.' I commit my body to You, Lord, and declare that it will remain undefiled.

2. Lord, I declare that I will flee from sexual immorality, as Your Word commands in 1 Corinthians 6:18: 'Flee sexual immorality. Every sin that a man does is outside the body, but he who commits sexual immorality sins against his own body.' I will run from temptation and refuse to entertain anything that leads me into sin.

3. I decree that I will walk in the Spirit and not fulfill the lust of the flesh, for Your Word says, 'Walk in the Spirit, and you shall not fulfill the lust of the
flesh' (Galatians 5:16). I align my thoughts, actions, and desires with the Spirit of God.

4. Father, I declare that I am sanctified and set apart for Your purpose. Your Word says, 'For this is the will of God, your sanctification: that you should abstain from sexual immorality' (1 Thessalonians 4:3). I choose sanctification over sin.

5. Lord, I rebuke every spirit of lust and declare that I am free, for Your Word says, 'If the Son makes you free, you shall be free indeed' (John 8:36). Lust has no power over me, and I walk in the liberty of Christ.

6. I declare that my thoughts are captive to the obedience of Christ, as written in 2 Corinthians 10:5: 'Casting down arguments and every high thing that exalts itself against the knowledge of God, bringing every thought into captivity to the obedience of Christ.' My mind is purified by Your Word.

7. Father, I decree that I will honor You with my eyes, for Your Word says, 'I have made a covenant with my eyes; why then should I look upon a young woman?' (Job 31:1). I reject every temptation to lust or entertain unholy images.

8. Lord, I declare that I will resist the devil, and he will flee from me, as written in James 4:7: 'Submit to God. Resist the devil and he will flee from you.' I submit myself to You, Lord, and reject every tactic of the enemy.

9. In the name of Jesus, I decree that I will not be conformed to this world but transformed by the renewing of my mind, as written in Romans 12:2. I reject the culture of compromise and embrace Your standard of holiness.

10. Father, I declare that I am clothed in the armor of light, as written in Romans 13:12-14: 'Let us cast off the works of darkness, and let us put on the armor of light... make no provision for the flesh, to fulfill its lusts.' I walk in Your light, and darkness has no place in me.

11. Lord, I decree that my relationships are governed by Your Word, for Your Word says, 'Do not be unequally yoked together with unbelievers. For what fellowship has righteousness with lawlessness?' (2 Corinthians 6:14). I align my relationships with Your standards.

12. I declare that I am filled with the fruit of self-control, for Your Word says, 'The fruit of the Spirit is love, joy, peace, longsuffering, kindness, goodness, faithfulness, gentleness, self-control' (Galatians 5:22-23). Self-control is my portion.

13. Father, I decree that I will guard my heart, for Your Word says, 'Above all else, guard your heart, for everything you do flows from it' (Proverbs 4:23, NIV). My heart is protected from lust, impurity, and compromise.

14. Lord, I declare that I will honor You in my relationships, for Your Word says, 'Marriage is honorable among all, and the bed undefiled; but fornicators and adulterers God will judge' (Hebrews 13:4). I commit to purity until marriage.

15. In the name of Jesus, I decree that I will not give the enemy a foothold, for Your Word says, 'Do not give the devil a foothold' (Ephesians 4:27, NIV). I close every door to sin and declare that I am protected by Your grace.

16. Father, I declare that I will walk in holiness, for Your Word says, 'Be holy, for I am holy' (1 Peter 1:16). My life is a reflection of Your holiness and glory.

17. Lord, I decree that I will abstain from temptation, for Your Word says, 'No temptation has overtaken you except such as is common to man; but God is faithful, who will not allow you to be tempted beyond what you are able' (1 Corinthians 10:13). I declare that You provide the strength to overcome.

18. I declare that my body is for the Lord, as written in 1

Corinthians 6:13: 'Now the body is not for sexual immorality but for the Lord, and the Lord for the body.' I offer my body as a living sacrifice to You.

19. Father, I rebuke every generational cycle of immorality and declare that I am free from the sins of my ancestors, for Your Word says, 'He who the Son sets free is free indeed' (John 8:36). I walk in purity and freedom.

20. Lord, I declare that I am strong in You and in the power of Your might, as written in Ephesians 6:10. I am empowered by Your Spirit to walk in purity and holiness all the days of my life.

**Closing Prayer:**

Father, I thank You for the gift of purity. As I declare these words, I receive the strength to walk in holiness, resist temptation, and honor You with my body, mind, and spirit. Let Your grace empower me daily to remain steadfast in my commitment to purity. I surrender my desires to You, trusting that You will fulfill them in Your perfect way and timing. In Jesus' name, Amen.

# CHAPTER 7

# Declarations for Boundaries with In-Laws

**Scripture Focus:**
*"For this reason, a man shall leave his father and mother and be joined to his wife, and the two shall become one flesh."*
*Ephesians 5:31 (NKJV)*

**Introduction:**
Marriage is a covenant between two people and God, yet it is surrounded by relationships that can either support or strain it. In-laws can be a blessing, offering wisdom, support, and encouragement. However, without clear boundaries, relationships with in-laws can become a source of tension, interference, or division. Boundaries are not barriers—they are safeguards that protect the integrity of the marriage covenant and foster healthy, respectful relationships.

God's design for marriage is clear: the two shall become one, leaving behind former dependencies to establish a new, united household (Ephesians 5:31). This chapter will empower you to set firm yet loving boundaries with in-laws, rebuke spirits of division or control, and align every relationship with God's purpose.

## 20 Declarations for Boundaries with In-Laws

1. Father, in the name of Jesus, I decree and declare that my marriage will be governed by Your Word, which says, 'For this reason, a man shall leave his father and mother and be joined to his wife, and the two shall become one flesh' (Ephesians 5:31). I declare that my spouse and I are united in spirit, purpose, and love.

2. Lord, I declare that I will honor my in-laws without compromising the unity of my marriage, as Your Word says, 'Honor your father and mother, which is the first commandment with promise' (Ephesians 6:2). I will walk in love and respect while maintaining healthy boundaries.

3. I decree that my marriage is protected from interference, for Your Word says, 'What therefore God has joined together, let not man separate' (Mark 10:9). No external relationship will undermine the covenant between me and my spouse.

4. Father, I declare that I am filled with wisdom to navigate relationships with in-laws. Your Word says, 'If any of you lacks wisdom, let him ask of God, who gives to all liberally and without reproach, and it will be given to him' (James 1:5). I receive divine wisdom to set boundaries in love.

5. Lord, I rebuke every spirit of control or manipulation that seeks to operate through in-laws. Your Word says, 'For God has not given us a spirit of fear, but of power and of love and of a sound mind' (2 Timothy 1:7). I declare freedom from fear and manipulation.

6. In the name of Jesus, I decree that every word spoken against my marriage by in-laws is nullified. Your Word says, 'No weapon formed against you shall prosper, and every tongue which rises against you in judgment you shall condemn' (Isaiah 54:17). I cancel every word of division or strife.

7. Father, I declare that I will walk in love and forgiveness, even when boundaries are tested. Your Word says, 'Be kind to one another, tenderhearted, forgiving one another, as God in Christ forgave you' (Ephesians 4:32). I choose love over resentment.

8. Lord, I decree that my spouse and I will communicate with one voice regarding our boundaries. Your Word says, 'Can two walk together, unless they are agreed?' (Amos 3:3). I declare unity in our decisions and mutual respect in our actions.

9. Father, I declare that I will not allow guilt to weaken my boundaries. Your Word says, 'For am I now seeking the approval of man, or of God? Or am I trying to please man? If I were still trying to please man, I would not be a servant of Christ' (Galatians 1:10). I seek to please You, Lord, above all else.

10. Lord, I decree that my in-laws will be a blessing to my marriage. Your Word says, 'Bless those who curse you, and pray for those who spitefully use you' (Luke 6:28). I speak blessings over them and declare that our relationship will reflect Your love.

11. Father, I rebuke every spirit of division that seeks to enter my marriage through in-laws. Your Word says, 'Every kingdom divided against itself is brought to desolation, and every city or

house divided against itself will not stand' (Matthew 12:25). I declare unity in my home.

12. Lord, I declare that I will not take offense but will operate in grace and truth. Your Word says, 'A person's wisdom yields patience; it is to one's glory to overlook an offense' (Proverbs 19:11, NIV). I choose patience and understanding in all interactions.

13. In the name of Jesus, I decree that my marriage is established in peace, for Your Word says, 'And the work of righteousness shall be peace; and the effect of righteousness quietness and assurance forever' (Isaiah 32:17). Peace rules in my home.

14. Father, I declare that my spouse and I are partners in building our home, as written in Proverbs 14:1: 'The wise woman builds her house, but with her own hands the foolish one tears hers down.' I will build wisely, guarding against external interference.

15. Lord, I decree that my words to my in-laws will be seasoned with grace, as Your Word says, 'Let your speech always be with grace, seasoned with salt, that you may know how you ought to answer each one' (Colossians 4:6). I will speak with kindness and wisdom.

16. Father, I rebuke every generational pattern of control, strife, or dysfunction. Your Word says, 'Therefore if anyone is in Christ, he is a new creation; old things have passed away; behold, all things have become new' (2 Corinthians 5:17). My marriage is a new creation in You.

17. Lord, I declare that I will uphold boundaries without fear, as Your Word says, 'The fear of man brings a snare, but whoever trusts in the Lord shall be safe' (Proverbs 29:25). I trust You to protect and guide my marriage.

18. In the name of Jesus, I decree that my spouse and I will honor our parents without allowing interference. Your Word says, 'Children, obey your parents in the Lord, for this is right. Honor your father and mother... that it may go well with you' (Ephesians 6:1-3). Honor and boundaries coexist in my home.

19. Father, I declare that You are my ultimate source of counsel and peace. Your Word says, 'For unto us a Child is born... and His name will be called Wonderful Counselor, Mighty God, Everlasting Father, Prince of Peace' (Isaiah 9:6). I rely on Your wisdom above all.

20. Lord, I decree and declare that my home is a sanctuary of unity, love, and protection. Your Word says, 'Unless the Lord builds the house, they labor in vain who build it' (Psalm 127:1). I invite You to build and establish my home.

**Closing Prayer:**
Father, I thank You for the gift of family and the blessings that come with unity. I declare that my marriage is covered by Your Word and protected from division or interference. Teach me to set boundaries in love and wisdom, ensuring that honor and respect prevail in all relationships. May my home reflect Your peace, unity, and presence. In Jesus' name, Amen.

# CHAPTER 8

# Declarations for the Little foxes

**Scripture Focus:**
*"Catch for us the foxes, the little foxes that ruin the vineyards, our vineyards that are in bloom."*
Song of Solomon 2:15 (NIV)

**Introduction:**
The little foxes are the small, seemingly insignificant issues that creep into relationships and wreak havoc if left unchecked. These can be habits, miscommunications, unspoken expectations, or subtle compromises that undermine trust and intimacy. While they may seem harmless at first, they have the potential to grow into major obstacles that destroy the fruit of your labor and love.

God desires to protect the "vineyard" of your future marriage and relationships. He equips you to recognize these foxes and deal with them before they cause damage. Through prayer, wisdom, and vigilance, you can uproot these issues and cultivate a relationship that thrives. This chapter will equip you with declarations to confront and conquer the little foxes, ensuring that your relationships bloom in righteousness and peace.

**20 Declarations for the Little Foxes**

1. Father, in the name of Jesus, I decree and declare that I am vigilant against the little foxes that seek to destroy the vineyard of my relationships. Your Word says, 'Catch for us the foxes, the little foxes that ruin the vineyards' (Song of Solomon 2:15). I declare that no hidden issue will go unchecked in my life.

2. Lord, I declare that I am clothed with the fruit of the Spirit, as written in Galatians 5:22-23: 'But the fruit of the Spirit is love, joy, peace, patience, kindness, goodness, faithfulness, gentleness, self-control.' These qualities guard my heart and relationships against subtle destruction.

3. I decree that my relationships are rooted in truth and honesty, for Your Word says, 'You desire truth in the inward parts, and in the hidden part You will make me to know wisdom' (Psalm 51:6). No deception or pretense will find a place in my life.

4. Father, I rebuke the fox of unspoken expectations. Your Word says, 'How can two walk together unless they agree?' (Amos 3:3). I declare clarity and communication in all my relationships.

5. Lord, I decree that the spirit of offense will not take root in my heart or relationships. Your Word says, 'Good sense makes one slow to anger, and it is his glory to overlook an offense' (Proverbs 19:11, ESV). I walk in patience and forgiveness.

6. In the name of Jesus, I declare that the fox of comparison is uprooted from my life. Your Word says, 'But let each one examine his own work, and then he will have rejoicing in himself alone,

and not in another' (Galatians 6:4). I am content with the path You have set for me.

7. Father, I declare that I will not allow miscommunication to destroy my relationships. Your Word says, 'Let your speech always be with grace, seasoned with salt, that you may know how you ought to answer each one' (Colossians 4:6). My words are guided by grace and wisdom.

8. Lord, I decree that bitterness and resentment have no power over me. Your Word says, 'Let all bitterness, wrath, anger, clamor, and evil speaking be put away from you, with all malice. And be kind to one another, tenderhearted, forgiving one another, even as God in Christ forgave you' (Ephesians 4:31-32). I walk in forgiveness and love.

9. I rebuke the fox of subtle compromise in my values. Your Word says, 'Do not be conformed to this world, but be transformed by the renewing of your
mind' (Romans 12:2). I hold fast to Your standards of righteousness.

10. Father, I decree that I will not allow pride to disrupt my relationships. Your Word says, 'Pride goes before destruction, and a haughty spirit before a fall' (Proverbs 16:18). I choose humility and grace.

11. Lord, I declare that I will address small issues before they grow into major problems. Your Word says, 'The prudent see danger and take refuge, but the simple keep going and pay the penalty' (Proverbs 22:3, NIV). I walk in wisdom and foresight.

12. I decree that my heart is guarded against the fox of jealousy. Your Word says, 'For where jealousy and selfish ambition exist, there will be disorder and every vile practice' (James 3:16). I walk in contentment and gratitude.

13. Father, I declare that I am quick to forgive, for Your Word says, 'Be angry, and do not sin; do not let the sun go down on your wrath, nor give place to the
devil' (Ephesians 4:26-27). I resolve conflicts quickly and in love.

14. Lord, I rebuke the fox of financial strife. Your Word says, 'The borrower is servant to the lender' (Proverbs 22:7). I declare financial wisdom and stewardship in my relationships.

15. I decree that my relationships are built on peace and not strife. Your Word says, 'Blessed are the peacemakers, for they shall be called sons of God' (Matthew 5:9). I am a peacemaker in all I do.

16. Father, I declare that I will not entertain gossip or negativity about others. Your Word says, 'A perverse person stirs up conflict, and a gossip separates close friends' (Proverbs 16:28, NIV). I reject gossip and walk in integrity.

17. Lord, I decree that I will guard my eyes, ears, and heart from influences that sow discord. Your Word says, 'Turn away from evil and do good; seek peace and pursue it' (Psalm 34:14). I pursue righteousness and peace.

18. I declare that I will recognize and uproot any fox of insecurity or self-doubt. Your Word says, 'For God has not given us a spirit

of fear, but of power and of love and of a sound mind' (2 Timothy 1:7). I walk in confidence and boldness.

19. Father, I rebuke the fox of past wounds and unhealed trauma. Your Word says, 'He heals the brokenhearted and binds up their wounds' (Psalm 147:3). I declare healing and wholeness in my heart.

20. Lord, I decree that my vineyard will flourish, for Your Word says, 'Those who are planted in the house of the Lord shall flourish in the courts of our God' (Psalm 92:13). My relationships will bear fruit and glorify You.

**Closing Prayer:**
Father, I thank You for the wisdom and grace to identify and uproot the little foxes in my life. Teach me to walk in vigilance, humility, and love, ensuring that my relationships flourish and reflect Your glory. Let every hidden issue be exposed and resolved through Your Spirit. I declare that my vineyard will thrive, untouched by the schemes of the enemy. In Jesus' name, Amen.

# CHAPTER 9

# Declarations Against Distraction

*Scripture Focus:*
*"Set your mind on things above, not on earthly things."*
*Colossians 3:2 (NIV)*

**Introduction:**
Distraction is one of the enemy's most effective weapons to derail your focus and divert your attention from God's purpose. Whether through misplaced priorities, unhealthy relationships, or overwhelming busyness, distractions can cause you to miss divine opportunities and delay your destiny.

To walk in alignment with God's plan, you must fix your heart and mind on Him. Colossians 3:2 reminds us to set our minds on things above, prioritizing His kingdom over temporary matters. These declarations will help you rebuke every distraction, sharpen your spiritual focus, and remain steadfast in your pursuit of God's will for your life.

# 20 Declarations Against Distraction

1. Father, in the name of Jesus, I decree and declare that my mind is set on things above and not on earthly distractions, as Your Word says in Colossians 3:2. My focus is fixed on Your will and purpose for my life.

2. Lord, I declare that I will not be entangled by the cares of this world, for Your Word says, 'No one engaged in warfare entangles himself with the affairs of this life, that he may please him who enlisted him as a soldier' (2 Timothy 2:4). I declare my commitment to Your mission.

3. I decree that every plan of the enemy to distract me from my calling is canceled. Your Word says, 'Submit to God. Resist the devil and he will flee from you' (James 4:7). I resist every scheme of the enemy in Jesus' name.

4. Father, I declare that my eyes are fixed on You, for Your Word says, 'Let us fix our eyes on Jesus, the author and finisher of our faith' (Hebrews 12:2). I will not be swayed by temporary concerns.

5. Lord, I rebuke every spirit of confusion that seeks to distract my mind. Your Word says, 'For God is not the author of confusion but of peace' (1 Corinthians 14:33). I declare clarity and peace in all I do.

6. In the name of Jesus, I decree that I will not be distracted by fear, for Your Word says, 'For God has not given us a spirit of fear, but of power and of love and of a sound mind' (2 Timothy 1:7). I walk in courage and boldness.

7. Father, I declare that I will discern between what is good and what is best. Your Word says, 'All things are lawful for me, but not all things are helpful' (1 Corinthians 10:23). I prioritize Your best for my life.

8. Lord, I decree that my relationships will not be a source of distraction. Your Word says, 'Do not be misled: "Bad company corrupts good character"' (1 Corinthians 15:33, NIV). I align myself with people who lead me closer to You.

9. Father, I declare that I will seek first Your kingdom and righteousness, for Your Word says, 'Seek first the kingdom of God and His righteousness, and all these things shall be added to you' (Matthew 6:33). I prioritize Your kingdom above all else.

10. In the name of Jesus, I decree that my time is redeemed, for Your Word says, 'See then that you walk circumspectly, not as fools but as wise, redeeming the time, because the days are evil' (Ephesians 5:15-16). I use my time wisely and purposefully.

11. Lord, I declare that my heart is undivided, for Your Word says, 'Teach me Your way, Lord, that I may rely on Your faithfulness; give me an undivided heart, that I may fear Your name' (Psalm 86:11, NIV). I commit my full attention to You.

12. Father, I decree that I will guard my mind from distractions, for Your Word says, 'Finally, brothers and sisters, whatever is true, whatever is noble, whatever is right, whatever is pure, whatever is lovely, whatever is admirable—if anything is excellent or praiseworthy—think about such things' (Philippians 4:8, NIV). My thoughts are focused on what is holy.

13. Lord, I declare that I will not be distracted by comparison. Your Word says, 'Each one should test their own actions. Then they can take pride in themselves alone, without comparing themselves to someone else' (Galatians 6:4, NIV). I celebrate my unique path in You.

14. Father, I rebuke every spirit of procrastination and declare that I will fulfill my assignments with diligence. Your Word says, 'The hand of the diligent will rule, but the lazy man will be put to forced labor' (Proverbs 12:24). I act promptly and with purpose.

15. In the name of Jesus, I declare that my priorities are aligned with Your will. Your Word says, 'Commit to the Lord whatever you do, and He will establish your plans' (Proverbs 16:3, NIV). I commit every task and decision to You.

16. Lord, I decree that I will not grow weary in doing good. Your Word says, 'And let us not grow weary while doing good, for in due season we shall reap if we do not lose heart' (Galatians 6:9). I press forward with perseverance.

17. Father, I declare that my mind is guarded against distractions, for Your Word says, 'You will keep him in perfect peace, whose mind is stayed on You, because he trusts in You' (Isaiah 26:3). My mind is steadfast in You.

18. Lord, I decree that I will focus on my divine assignment, for Your Word says, 'But one thing I do: Forgetting what is behind and straining toward what is ahead, I press on toward the goal to win the prize for which God has called me heavenward in Christ Jesus' (Philippians 3:13-14, NIV). I remain focused on my heavenly goal.

19. Father, I rebuke every attempt of the enemy to divert my focus. Your Word says, 'The thief does not come except to steal, and to kill, and to destroy. I have come that they may have life, and that they may have it more abundantly' (John 10:10). I choose the abundant life in Christ.

20. In the name of Jesus, I declare that I am focused and unwavering. Your Word says, 'Be steadfast, immovable, always abounding in the work of the Lord, knowing that your labor is not in vain in the Lord' (1 Corinthians 15:58). I stand firm in my purpose.

**Closing Prayer:**
Father, I thank You for the ability to remain steadfast in You. Let every distraction be removed, and let my mind, heart, and spirit be fully aligned with Your will. Teach me to discern what is truly important and give me the strength to pursue it with diligence and focus. I declare that my life will glorify You, free from distraction, as I walk in Your divine purpose. In Jesus' name, Amen.

# CHAPTER 10

# Declarations for Guarding the Heart

**Scripture Focus:**
*"Above all else, guard your heart, for everything you do flows from it."*
*Proverbs 4:23 (NIV)*

**Introduction:**
The heart is the seat of your emotions, decisions, and desires, and it must be protected with vigilance. An unguarded heart is vulnerable to offense, bitterness, distraction, and sin. Proverbs 4:23 reminds us that everything flows from the heart—your relationships, your purpose, and your ability to love and trust God.

To guard your heart is to set boundaries, filter influences, and cultivate a spirit of discernment. It is an act of worship and obedience, ensuring that nothing impure or harmful takes root in the place where God dwells. These declarations will help you protect your heart from the attacks of the enemy, align your desires with God's will, and cultivate a spirit of peace and love.

## 20 Declarations for Guarding the Heart

1. Father, in the name of Jesus, I decree and declare that my heart is guarded by Your peace, for Your Word says, 'Above all else, guard your heart, for everything you do flows from it' (Proverbs 4:23). I surrender my heart to You and trust You to protect it.

2. Lord, I declare that I will not allow offense to take root in my heart, for Your Word says, 'A person's wisdom yields patience; it is to one's glory to overlook an offense' (Proverbs 19:11, NIV). I release every offense and choose to walk in forgiveness.

3. I decree that my heart is filled with peace, for Your Word says, 'Let the peace of Christ rule in your hearts, since as members of one body you were called to peace' (Colossians 3:15, NIV). I allow Your peace to reign in me.

4. Father, I declare that my heart is purified by Your Word, for Your Word says, 'How can a young man keep his way pure? By guarding it according to Your Word' (Psalm 119:9, ESV). I meditate on Your Word day and night.

5. Lord, I rebuke every spirit of bitterness and declare that my heart is filled with love. Your Word says, 'Get rid of all bitterness, rage and anger, brawling and slander, along with every form of malice. Be kind and compassionate to one another, forgiving each other, just as in Christ God forgave you' (Ephesians 4:31-32, NIV). I choose kindness and forgiveness.

6. In the name of Jesus, I decree that my heart is not troubled or afraid, for Your Word says, 'Do not let your hearts be troubled. You believe in God; believe also in Me' (John 14:1, NIV). I walk in faith and trust in You.

7. Father, I declare that I will guard my heart against negativity and doubt. Your Word says, 'Finally, brothers and sisters, whatever is true, whatever is noble, whatever is right, whatever is pure, whatever is lovely, whatever is admirable—if anything is excellent or praiseworthy—think about such things' (Philippians 4:8, NIV). My thoughts are fixed on You.

8. Lord, I decree that my heart is a dwelling place for Your Spirit. Your Word says, 'Do you not know that you are God's temple and that God's Spirit dwells in you?' (1 Corinthians 3:16, ESV). I declare that my heart is holy ground.

9. Father, I rebuke every lie of the enemy that seeks to corrupt my heart. Your Word says, 'The thief does not come except to steal, and to kill, and to destroy. I have come that they may have life, and that they may have it more abundantly' (John 10:10). I embrace Your abundant life.

10. Lord, I declare that my heart is aligned with Your will. Your Word says, 'Create in me a clean heart, O God, and renew a steadfast spirit within me' (Psalm 51:10). Purify my heart and renew my spirit.

11. I decree that my heart is guarded against fear, for Your Word says, 'Perfect love casts out fear, because fear has to do with

punishment. The one who fears is not made perfect in love' (1 John 4:18, NIV). I rest in Your perfect love.

12. Father, I declare that my heart will not be deceived, for Your Word says, 'The heart is deceitful above all things, and desperately sick; who can understand it? I the Lord search the heart and test the mind' (Jeremiah 17:9-10, ESV). I submit my heart to Your examination.

13. Lord, I decree that my heart is filled with joy, for Your Word says, 'A joyful heart is good medicine, but a crushed spirit dries up the bones' (Proverbs 17:22, ESV). I declare that joy is my portion.

14. Father, I declare that I will guard my heart from unhealthy influences. Your Word says, 'Do not be misled: "Bad company corrupts good character"' (1 Corinthians 15:33, NIV). I choose relationships that nurture my spirit.

15. Lord, I decree that my heart is steadfast in You. Your Word says, 'My heart is steadfast, O God, my heart is steadfast; I will sing and make melody!' (Psalm 57:7, ESV). I remain unwavering in my faith.

16. Father, I declare that my heart is not weighed down by worry, for Your Word says, 'Cast all your anxiety on Him because He cares for you' (1 Peter 5:7, NIV). I release my burdens to You.

17. Lord, I rebuke the seeds of unforgiveness in my heart. Your Word says, 'Forgive, and you will be forgiven' (Luke 6:37, NIV). I choose forgiveness over resentment.

18. Father, I decree that my heart is shielded by Your Word, for Your Word says, 'Your Word I have hidden in my heart, that I might not sin against You' (Psalm 119:11). I treasure Your Word in my heart.

19. Lord, I declare that my heart is aligned with Your love, for Your Word says, 'Love the Lord your God with all your heart and with all your soul and with all your mind' (Matthew 22:37, NIV). I commit my entire being to You.

20. In the name of Jesus, I decree that my heart will remain pure, peaceful, and aligned with Your purpose. Your Word says, 'Blessed are the pure in heart, for they shall see God' (Matthew 5:8, ESV). I declare that I will see You, Lord, in all areas of my life.

**Closing Prayer:**
Father, I thank You for guarding my heart against anything that seeks to defile or distract me. I submit my heart, mind, and spirit to You, trusting that You will purify and protect me. Help me to walk in love, forgiveness, and purity, reflecting Your glory in all I do. In Jesus' name, Amen.

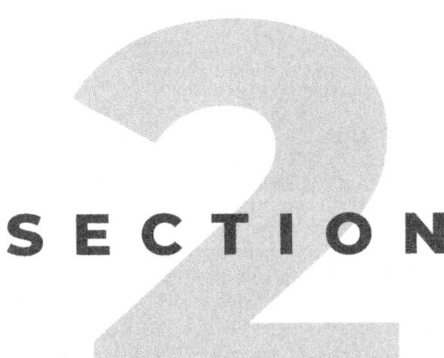

# SECTION 2

# SPIRITUAL WARFARE AND SEXUAL PURITY

# CHAPTER 11

# Declarations for Becoming a Virtuous Woman

**Scripture Focus:**
*"Who can find a virtuous woman? For her price is far above rubies."*
*Proverbs 31:10 (KJV)*

**Introduction:**
A virtuous woman is a treasure in the sight of God and man. She is strong, wise, faithful, and a blessing to all who encounter her. Becoming a virtuous woman is not merely about outward behavior but about an inward transformation that reflects the heart of Christ.

Proverbs 31 outlines the characteristics of a virtuous woman, showing her to be industrious, wise, compassionate, and a source of honor for her household. This chapter will guide you in declaring God's promises over your life, shaping your heart, mind, and actions to align with His divine design for you as a virtuous woman.

# 20 Declarations for Becoming a Virtuous Woman

1. Father, in the name of Jesus, I decree and declare that I am becoming a virtuous woman, for Your Word says, 'Who can find a virtuous woman? For her price is far above rubies' (Proverbs 31:10). I embrace my worth in You, knowing I am valued far beyond measure.

2. Lord, I declare that I walk in strength and dignity, as Your Word says, 'She is clothed with strength and dignity; she can laugh at the days to come' (Proverbs 31:25, NIV). I declare that fear has no place in my future.

3. I decree that my words are filled with wisdom, for Your Word says, 'She opens her mouth with wisdom, and the teaching of kindness is on her tongue' (Proverbs 31:26). I speak life, encouragement, and truth in all I say.

4. Father, I declare that I am diligent in all I do, for Your Word says, 'She watches over the affairs of her household and does not eat the bread of idleness' (Proverbs 31:27). I rebuke laziness and embrace diligence and responsibility.

5. Lord, I decree that I bring good to others, for Your Word says, 'She brings him good, not harm, all the days of her life' (Proverbs 31:12, NIV). I commit to being a source of blessing and not a cause of harm.

6. In the name of Jesus, I declare that I am clothed in compassion, for Your Word says, 'She extends her hand to the poor, yes, she reaches out her hands to the needy' (Proverbs 31:20). I will serve others with love and generosity.

7. Father, I decree that I am strong in faith, for Your Word says, 'She girds herself with strength, and strengthens her arms' (Proverbs 31:17). I declare that I am spiritually strong and prepared for every challenge.

8. Lord, I declare that I build my home with wisdom, for Your Word says, 'The wise woman builds her house, but with her own hands the foolish one tears hers down' (Proverbs 14:1). I am a wise steward of my home and relationships.

9. Father, I decree that I fear You above all, for Your Word says, 'Charm is deceitful and beauty is passing, but a woman who fears the Lord, she shall be
praised' (Proverbs 31:30). My reverence for You is the foundation of my life.

10. Lord, I declare that I am a prudent and discerning woman, for Your Word says, 'The prudent see danger and take refuge, but the simple keep going and pay the penalty' (Proverbs 22:3, NIV). I make decisions with wisdom and foresight.

11. Father, I decree that I manage resources wisely, for Your Word says, 'She considers a field and buys it; from her profits, she plants a vineyard' (Proverbs 31:16). I am a wise steward of all You have entrusted to me.

12. Lord, I declare that my hands are productive, for Your Word says, 'She seeks wool and flax and willingly works with her hands' (Proverbs 31:13). I am diligent and fruitful in all I do.

13. In the name of Jesus, I decree that my life is marked by

kindness and love. Your Word says, 'Let all that you do be done with love' (1 Corinthians 16:14). I act in love in all my relationships.

14. Father, I declare that I am a pillar of strength in my family and community. Your Word says, 'She perceives that her merchandise is good, and her lamp does not go out by night' (Proverbs 31:18). I shine brightly in every season.

15. Lord, I decree that I am an encourager and supporter of others, for Your Word says, 'Therefore encourage one another and build each other up' (1 Thessalonians 5:11, NIV). I speak words that uplift and inspire.

16. Father, I declare that I reflect Your glory in all I do. Your Word says, 'But we all, with unveiled face, beholding as in a mirror the glory of the Lord, are being transformed into the same image from glory to glory' (2 Corinthians 3:18). My life glorifies You, Lord.

17. Lord, I decree that I am a woman of faith, hope, and perseverance. Your Word says, 'Blessed is she who has believed that the Lord would fulfill His promises to
her' (Luke 1:45, NIV). I stand firm in faith, knowing You are faithful.

18. Father, I declare that I am an excellent example to others, for Your Word says, 'In everything set them an example by doing what is good. In your teaching show integrity, seriousness, and soundness of speech that cannot be condemned' (Titus 2:7-8, NIV). My life is a testimony of Your goodness.

19. Lord, I decree that I am confident in who You have made me to be. Your Word says, 'For we are His workmanship, created in Christ Jesus for good works, which God prepared beforehand that we should walk in them' (Ephesians 2:10). I walk boldly in my purpose.

20. Father, I declare that I am a virtuous woman who reflects Your character. Your Word says, 'Strength and honor are her clothing; she shall rejoice in time to come' (Proverbs 31:25). I am clothed in Your strength and honor.

**Closing Prayer:**
Father, I thank You for calling me to be a virtuous woman. As I declare these truths over my life, transform my heart, mind, and actions to align with Your Word. Teach me to walk in wisdom, strength, and love, bringing glory to Your name in all I do. Let my life be a testimony of Your grace and a blessing to all around me. In Jesus' name, Amen.

# CHAPTER 12

## Declarations for Becoming a Valorous Husband

*Scripture Focus:*
*"Husbands, love your wives, just as Christ also loved the church and gave Himself for her."*
*Ephesians 5:25 (NKJV)*

**Introduction:**
A valorous husband is a man of honor, strength, and love, modeling Christ's relationship with the Church in his marriage. His love is sacrificial, his leadership is servant-hearted, and his commitment to his family is unwavering. Becoming a valorous husband begins long before marriage—it starts with cultivating a heart that reflects the character of Christ.

Ephesians 5:25 calls husbands to love their wives with the same selflessness and devotion that Christ demonstrated for His bride. This chapter equips you to declare God's promises over your life as you prepare to step into the role of a godly husband. These declarations will shape your character, refine your leadership, and align your actions with God's design for biblical manhood.

## 20 Declarations for Becoming a Valorous Husband

1. Father, in the name of Jesus, I decree and declare that I will love my future wife as Christ loves the Church, for Your Word says, 'Husbands, love your wives, just as Christ also loved the church and gave Himself for her' (Ephesians 5:25). I commit to sacrificial, unconditional love.

2. Lord, I declare that I will lead my household with wisdom and humility. Your Word says, 'The husband is the head of the wife, as Christ is the head of the church' (Ephesians 5:23). I embrace this responsibility with reverence and integrity.

3. I decree that I am a protector of my family, for Your Word says, 'Be strong and courageous. Do not be afraid; do not be discouraged, for the Lord your God will be with you wherever you go' (Joshua 1:9, NIV). I stand as a shield of strength for my household.

4. Father, I declare that I will provide for my family, as Your Word says, 'But if anyone does not provide for his own, and especially for those of his household, he has denied the faith and is worse than an unbeliever' (1 Timothy 5:8). I walk in diligence and responsibility.

5. Lord, I decree that I will nurture my wife spiritually, for Your Word says, 'Sanctify her, cleansing her by the washing with water through the word' (Ephesians 5:26, NIV). I will lead with prayer and the Word of God.

6. In the name of Jesus, I declare that I will honor my wife, for Your Word says, 'Husbands, likewise, dwell with them with understanding, giving honor to the wife, as to the weaker vessel, and as being heirs together of the grace of life' (1 Peter 3:7). I will treat her with respect and tenderness.

7. Father, I decree that I will be patient and kind in all my dealings, for Your Word says, 'Love is patient, love is kind. It does not envy, it does not boast, it is not proud' (1 Corinthians 13:4, NIV). I will reflect Your love in my actions.

8. Lord, I declare that I will guard my eyes and heart from temptation. Your Word says, 'I have made a covenant with my eyes; why then should I look upon a young woman?' (Job 31:1). I will remain faithful in thought and deed.

9. Father, I decree that I will lay down my pride and serve my wife with humility. Your Word says, 'Whoever wants to become great among you must be your
servant' (Matthew 20:26, NIV). I will lead by serving.

10. Lord, I declare that I will be slow to anger and quick to listen. Your Word says, 'Everyone should be quick to listen, slow to speak and slow to become angry' (James 1:19, NIV). I will approach every situation with grace and understanding.

11. Father, I decree that I will be faithful and trustworthy, for Your Word says, 'A faithful man will abound with blessings' (Proverbs 28:20). My commitment to my wife will never waver.

12. Lord, I declare that I will protect the unity of my marriage.

Your Word says, 'Therefore what God has joined together, let no one separate' (Mark 10:9, NIV). I rebuke every spirit of division in Jesus' name.

13. In the name of Jesus, I decree that I will teach my children to walk in Your ways, for Your Word says, 'Train up a child in the way he should go, and when he is old he will not depart from it' (Proverbs 22:6). I will be an example of godliness in my home.

14. Father, I declare that I will walk in forgiveness, for Your Word says, 'Bear with each other and forgive one another if any of you has a grievance against someone. Forgive as the Lord forgave you' (Colossians 3:13, NIV). I will extend grace in every circumstance.

15. Lord, I decree that I will communicate with love and wisdom, for Your Word says, 'Let your speech always be gracious, seasoned with salt, so that you may know how you ought to answer each person' (Colossians 4:6, ESV). My words will build up and not tear down.

16. Father, I declare that I will cultivate a spirit of gratitude in my marriage. Your Word says, 'In everything give thanks; for this is the will of God in Christ Jesus for you' (1 Thessalonians 5:18). I will honor You with a heart of thanksgiving.

17. Lord, I decree that I will walk in courage and faith, for Your Word says, 'Be on your guard; stand firm in the faith; be courageous; be strong' (1 Corinthians 16:13, NIV). I will face every challenge with confidence in You.

18. Father, I declare that I will create an atmosphere of peace in my home. Your Word says, 'Blessed are the peacemakers, for they shall be called sons of God' (Matthew 5:9). I will pursue peace in every situation.

19. Lord, I decree that I will model Christlike leadership, for Your Word says, 'For even the Son of Man did not come to be served, but to serve, and to give His life as a ransom for many' (Mark 10:45, NIV). My leadership will reflect Your love and sacrifice.

20. Father, I declare that I am a man of valor, strength, and integrity, ready to fulfill the role of a godly husband. Your Word says, 'The righteous man walks in his integrity; his children are blessed after him' (Proverbs 20:7). I walk in righteousness and integrity.

**Closing Prayer:**
Father, I thank You for calling me to be a man of valor, prepared to love, lead, and serve as a godly husband. Transform my heart and shape my character to reflect Christ in all I do.
Strengthen me to honor my future wife, protect my family, and glorify You in my marriage. I surrender every area of my life to You, trusting that You will guide me as I walk this journey. In Jesus' name, Amen.

# CHAPTER 13

# Declarations for Financial Provision and Generational Wealth

***Scripture Focus:***
*"But remember the Lord your God, for it is He who gives you the ability to produce wealth, and so confirms His covenant."*
*Deuteronomy 8:18 (NIV)*

**Introduction:**
Financial provision and generational wealth are part of God's covenant promises. While wealth is not the sole measure of success, it is a tool for fulfilling His purposes and blessing others. God desires that His children live in abundance, free from financial stress, and equipped to leave an inheritance for future generations.

Proverbs 13:22 says, "A good man leaves an inheritance to his children's children," emphasizing the importance of stewardship and long-term vision. These declarations will empower you to partner with God for supernatural provision, break cycles of financial lack, and build a legacy that glorifies Him.

## 20 Declarations for Financial Provision and Generational Wealth

1. Father, in the name of Jesus, I decree and declare that You are my ultimate provider, for Your Word says, 'And my God shall supply all your need according to His riches in glory by Christ Jesus' (Philippians 4:19). I trust in Your abundant provision.

2. Lord, I declare that I have the power to create wealth, for Your Word says, 'But remember the Lord your God, for it is He who gives you the ability to produce wealth' (Deuteronomy 8:18). I walk in divine creativity and resourcefulness.

3. I decree that I will not live in lack, for Your Word says, 'The Lord is my shepherd; I shall not want' (Psalm 23:1). I declare that every need in my life is met in abundance.

4. Father, I declare that I am a wise steward of the resources You entrust to me. Your Word says, 'It is required in stewards that one be found faithful' (1 Corinthians 4:2). I will manage my finances with wisdom and integrity.

5. Lord, I decree that I will leave a legacy of wealth, for Your Word says, 'A good man leaves an inheritance to his children's children' (Proverbs 13:22). I declare that my wealth will bless generations.

6. In the name of Jesus, I rebuke every spirit of poverty and declare that I walk in abundance. Your Word says, 'Beloved, I pray that you may prosper in all things and be in health, just as your soul prospers' (3 John 1:2).

7. Father, I decree that I will honor You with my finances, for Your Word says, 'Honor the Lord with your possessions, and with the firstfruits of all your increase; so your barns will be filled with plenty, and your vats will overflow with new wine' (Proverbs 3:9-10). I commit to giving generously.

8. Lord, I declare that You are opening doors of financial opportunity, for Your Word says, 'I have set before you an open door, and no one can shut it' (Revelation 3:8). I step into new realms of provision.

9. Father, I rebuke the devourer from my finances, for Your Word says, 'And I will rebuke the devourer for your sakes, so that he will not destroy the fruit of your ground' (Malachi 3:11). I declare that my resources are protected.

10. In the name of Jesus, I decree that my hands are blessed. Your Word says, 'The Lord will open the heavens, the storehouse of His bounty, to send rain on your land in season and to bless all the work of your hands' (Deuteronomy 28:12). My labor is fruitful and prosperous.

11. Lord, I declare that I will not be anxious about finances, for Your Word says, 'Do not worry, saying, "What shall we eat?" or "What shall we drink?"... But seek first the kingdom of God and His righteousness, and all these things shall be added to you' (Matthew 6:31-33). My focus is on Your kingdom.

12. Father, I decree that I will lend and not borrow, for Your Word says, 'The Lord will make you the head and not the tail; you shall

be above only, and not be beneath' (Deuteronomy 28:13). I walk in financial dominion.

13. Lord, I declare that my wealth will glorify You. Your Word says, 'Command those who are rich in this present age not to be haughty, nor to trust in uncertain riches but in the living God, who gives us richly all things to enjoy' (1 Timothy 6:17). I trust in You, not in riches.

14. Father, I decree that every seed I sow will yield a bountiful harvest, for Your Word says, 'He who sows sparingly will also reap sparingly, and he who sows bountifully will also reap bountifully' (2 Corinthians 9:6). I sow generously and with faith.

15. Lord, I rebuke the spirit of financial fear. Your Word says, 'For God has not given us a spirit of fear, but of power and of love and of a sound mind' (2 Timothy 1:7). I walk in confidence in Your provision.

16. Father, I declare that I will invest wisely and with discernment. Your Word says, 'The plans of the diligent lead surely to plenty, but those of everyone who is hasty, surely to poverty' (Proverbs 21:5). I plan and execute with care.

17. Lord, I decree that my wealth will be a blessing to others. Your Word says, 'It is more blessed to give than to receive' (Acts 20:35). I commit to generosity and compassion.

18. Father, I declare that You are enlarging my territory. Your Word says, 'Oh, that You would bless me indeed, and enlarge my territory, that Your hand would be with me' (1 Chronicles 4:10). I step into greater influence and provision.

19. In the name of Jesus, I decree that I will not grow weary in financial stewardship. Your Word says, 'And let us not grow weary while doing good, for in due season we shall reap if we do not lose heart' (Galatians 6:9). I persevere in diligence.

20. Lord, I declare that I will seek You above all else. Your Word says, 'But you shall remember the Lord your God, for it is He who gives you power to get wealth' (Deuteronomy 8:18). I rely on Your wisdom and strength to build wealth for Your glory.

**Closing Prayer:**
Father, I thank You for being the source of all provision and wealth. Teach me to steward my resources with wisdom and align my financial goals with Your purposes. I rebuke every spirit of poverty and lack and declare that I will walk in abundance, leaving a legacy of wealth for generations to come. Let my financial journey bring glory to Your name and expand Your kingdom. In Jesus' name, Amen.

# CHAPTER 14

# Declarations to Satan-Proof Your Marriage

***Scripture Focus:***
*"Though one may be overpowered, two can defend themselves.
A cord of three strands is not quickly broken."
Ecclesiastes 4:12 (NIV)*

**Introduction:**

Marriage is a covenant designed by God, but it is constantly under attack by the enemy. Satan seeks to sow discord, division, and destruction within families, knowing that strong marriages build strong homes, communities, and nations. To satan-proof your marriage is to cover it with prayer, align it with God's Word, and stand united against every scheme of the enemy.

Ecclesiastes 4:12 reminds us that a marriage anchored in Christ is unbreakable—a threefold cord that cannot easily be undone. These declarations will help you fortify your marriage, rebuke the enemy's attacks, and establish your relationship on the solid foundation of God's truth.

## 20 Declarations to Satan-Proof Your Marriage

1. Father, in the name of Jesus, I decree and declare that my marriage is built on the Rock, for Your Word says, 'Therefore everyone who hears these words of mine and puts them into practice is like a wise man who built his house on the rock' (Matthew 7:24). My marriage is immovable in Christ.

2. Lord, I declare that my spouse and I are united in spirit and purpose, for Your Word says, 'If a house is divided against itself, that house cannot stand' (Mark 3:25). I rebuke division and declare unity in our home.

3. I decree that every plan of the enemy against my marriage is canceled. Your Word says, 'No weapon formed against you shall prosper, and every tongue which rises against you in judgment you shall condemn' (Isaiah 54:17). My marriage is covered by Your protection.

4. Father, I declare that my marriage is a reflection of Christ's love for the Church, for Your Word says, 'Husbands, love your wives, just as Christ loved the church and gave Himself up for her' (Ephesians 5:25). Our love is sacrificial and enduring.

5. Lord, I decree that my marriage is filled with peace and joy, for Your Word says, 'May the God of hope fill you with all joy and peace as you trust in Him' (Romans 15:13, NIV). I declare an atmosphere of peace in our home.

6. In the name of Jesus, I rebuke every spirit of strife and

contention. Your Word says, 'A gentle answer turns away wrath, but a harsh word stirs up anger' (Proverbs 15:1, NIV). I declare gentleness and understanding in all communication.

7. Father, I declare that forgiveness flows freely in my marriage, for Your Word says, 'Be kind to one another, tenderhearted, forgiving one another, as God in Christ forgave you' (Ephesians 4:32). We walk in grace and mercy.

8. Lord, I decree that my spouse and I will resist temptation and remain faithful. Your Word says, 'No temptation has overtaken you except what is common to mankind. And God is faithful; He will not let you be tempted beyond what you can bear' (1 Corinthians 10:13, NIV). We stand firm against every snare.

9. Father, I rebuke every spirit of offense that seeks to take root in our hearts. Your Word says, 'Good sense makes one slow to anger, and it is his glory to overlook an offense' (Proverbs 19:11, ESV). I declare that we choose forgiveness over bitterness.

10. In the name of Jesus, I decree that my marriage is guarded by prayer. Your Word says, 'Pray without ceasing' (1 Thessalonians 5:17). We cover our union with intercession daily.

11. Lord, I declare that my spouse and I will submit to one another in love, for Your Word says, 'Submit to one another out of reverence for Christ' (Ephesians 5:21). We honor each other in humility.

12. Father, I decree that my home is filled with Your presence, for

Your Word says, 'Unless the Lord builds the house, the builders labor in vain' (Psalm 127:1, NIV). I invite You to be the center of our marriage

13. Lord, I rebuke the spirit of jealousy and declare trust in my marriage. Your Word says, 'Love is patient, love is kind... It does not envy, it does not boast, it is not proud' (1 Corinthians 13:4, NIV). I declare that love rules in our hearts.

14. Father, I declare that my marriage is fruitful in every way. Your Word says, 'God blessed them and said to them, "Be fruitful and increase in number; fill the earth and subdue it"' (Genesis 1:28). I declare fruitfulness in our union.

15. Lord, I decree that my spouse and I will not allow the sun to go down on our anger, for Your Word says, 'Do not let the sun go down while you are still angry, and do not give the devil a foothold' (Ephesians 4:26-27, NIV). We resolve conflicts quickly and in love.

16. Father, I declare that we are yoked together in Christ, for Your Word says, 'Do not be unequally yoked with unbelievers' (2 Corinthians 6:14). Our relationship is rooted in mutual faith.

17. Lord, I decree that my marriage is a light to others, for Your Word says, 'You are the light of the world. A town built on a hill cannot be hidden' (Matthew 5:14, NIV). We reflect Your glory in our love.

18. Father, I rebuke every generational curse that seeks to affect my marriage. Your Word says, 'Christ redeemed us from the

curse of the law by becoming a curse for us' (Galatians 3:13, NIV). I declare that we walk in freedom and blessing.

19. Lord, I decree that my spouse and I will walk in agreement, for Your Word says, 'Can two walk together unless they are agreed?' (Amos 3:3). We are united in vision, purpose, and love.

20. Father, I declare that my marriage is a threefold cord, as written in Ecclesiastes 4:12: 'Though one may be overpowered, two can defend themselves. A cord of three strands is not quickly broken.' You are the center of our union, and we will not be shaken.

**Closing Prayer:**
Father, I thank You for the covenant of marriage and the divine protection You provide. I declare that no weapon formed against my union will prosper. Strengthen us to walk in love, humility, and unity. Teach us to guard our marriage with prayer, wisdom, and discernment. May our relationship reflect Your glory and stand as a testimony of Your faithfulness. In Jesus' name, Amen.

# CHAPTER 15

## Declarations for Engagement Warfare

**Scripture Focus:**
*"For we do not wrestle against flesh and blood, but against principalities, against powers, against the rulers of the darkness of this age."*
*Ephesians 6:12 (NKJV)*

**Introduction:**
Engagement is not just a step toward marriage; it is a spiritual battleground. The enemy often intensifies his attacks during this season, sowing seeds of doubt, fear, and discord to disrupt what God has ordained. Engagement warfare is about standing firm in faith, covering your relationship with prayer, and dismantling every spiritual attack.

Ephesians 6:12 reminds us that the battle is not against flesh and blood but against spiritual forces. This chapter equips you with powerful declarations to guard your engagement, rebuke the enemy, and prepare for a marriage that glorifies God.

# 20 Declarations for Engagement Warfare

1. Father, in the name of Jesus, I decree and declare that my engagement is covered by the blood of Jesus. Your Word says, 'They overcame him by the blood of the Lamb and by the word of their testimony' (Revelation 12:11). No weapon formed against us will prosper.

2. Lord, I declare that my engagement is a season of preparation, not destruction. Your Word says, 'For I know the plans I have for you, declares the Lord, plans for welfare and not for evil, to give you a future and a hope' (Jeremiah 29:11, ESV). I trust Your plans for our union.

3. I decree that every spirit of confusion and division is rebuked in Jesus' name. Your Word says, 'For God is not the author of confusion but of peace' (1 Corinthians 14:33). I declare peace over this season.

4. Father, I declare that my engagement is anchored in truth and love, for Your Word says, 'Love does not delight in evil but rejoices with the truth' (1 Corinthians 13:6, NIV). I rebuke every lie and deception.

5. Lord, I decree that fear will not rule my heart, for Your Word says, 'There is no fear in love, but perfect love casts out fear' (1 John 4:18). I walk in confidence and boldness.

6. In the name of Jesus, I declare that my fiancé and I are united in spirit and purpose. Your Word says, 'Make every effort to keep the unity of the Spirit through the bond of peace' (Ephesians 4:3, NIV). We are bound together in harmony.

7. Father, I rebuke every spirit of doubt and declare faith over my engagement. Your Word says, 'Now faith is the substance of things hoped for, the evidence of things not seen' (Hebrews 11:1). I declare unwavering trust in You.

8. Lord, I decree that my engagement is protected from spiritual attacks. Your Word says, 'The Lord is faithful, and He will strengthen you and protect you from the evil one' (2 Thessalonians 3:3, NIV). I declare divine protection.

9. Father, I declare that my fiancé and I will pray together and seek Your will, for Your Word says, 'For where two or three gather in My name, there am I with
them' (Matthew 18:20). Your presence is central to our relationship.

10. In the name of Jesus, I decree that every generational curse is broken. Your Word says, 'Christ redeemed us from the curse of the law by becoming a curse for
us' (Galatians 3:13). Our engagement is free from the burdens of the past.

11. Lord, I declare that the foundation of our relationship is Christ, for Your Word says, 'For no one can lay any foundation other than the one already laid, which is Jesus Christ' (1 Corinthians 3:11, NIV). Our love is rooted in You.

12. Father, I rebuke every spirit of offense and declare forgiveness in our relationship. Your Word says, 'Be kind and compassionate to one another, forgiving each other, just as in Christ God forgave you' (Ephesians 4:32, NIV). We choose grace over conflict.

13. Lord, I decree that our engagement is a testimony of Your faithfulness. Your Word says, 'The one who calls you is faithful, and He will do it' (1 Thessalonians 5:24, NIV). Our story reflects Your glory.

14. In the name of Jesus, I declare that no spirit of manipulation or control will infiltrate our relationship. Your Word says, 'Where the Spirit of the Lord is, there is freedom' (2 Corinthians 3:17). We walk in liberty and truth.

15. Father, I declare that every negative word spoken against our engagement is nullified. Your Word says, 'No weapon formed against you shall prosper, and every tongue which rises against you in judgment you shall condemn' (Isaiah 54:17). I silence every attack.

16. Lord, I decree that we are equipped for spiritual warfare. Your Word says, 'Put on the full armor of God, so that you can take your stand against the devil's
schemes' (Ephesians 6:11, NIV). We stand firm in Your power.

17. Father, I declare that my engagement is surrounded by godly counsel, for Your Word says, 'Where there is no guidance, a people falls, but in an abundance of counselors there is safety' (Proverbs 11:14, ESV). We seek wisdom and support.

18. In the name of Jesus, I decree that every spirit of delay and distraction is broken. Your Word says, 'The Lord will fight for you; you need only to be still' (Exodus 14:14, NIV). I declare progress and clarity in this season.

19. Lord, I declare that we are preparing for a marriage that reflects Your kingdom. Your Word says, 'Your kingdom come, Your will be done, on earth as it is in heaven' (Matthew 6:10). Our union is a testimony of heaven on earth.

20. Father, I decree that our engagement is covered in prayer, love, and faith. Your Word says, 'Pray in the Spirit on all occasions with all kinds of prayers and requests' (Ephesians 6:18, NIV). We commit this season to You, Lord.

**Closing Prayer:**
Father, I thank You for the sacred season of engagement. I declare that every weapon of the enemy is dismantled and every plan of Yours is established. Teach us to walk in faith, unity, and love, preparing for a marriage that honors You. Surround us with Your peace and protect us from every attack. Let our engagement glorify You and serve as a witness of Your faithfulness. In Jesus' name, Amen.

# CHAPTER 16

# Declarations for the Wedding Day

**Scripture Focus:**
*"This is the day that the Lord has made;
let us rejoice and be glad in it."
Psalm 118:24 (ESV)*

**Introduction:**
The wedding day is not just a celebration of love but a sacred covenant made before God and witnesses. It is a day of great spiritual significance, marking the beginning of a lifelong journey together. While it is a joyful occasion, it is also a target for spiritual distractions and anxiety.

Psalm 118:24 reminds us to rejoice and be glad, as the Lord orchestrates this day. These declarations will help you to cover every aspect of the wedding day in prayer, ensure a spirit of peace and joy, and dedicate this milestone to the glory of God.

# 20 Declarations for the Wedding Day

1. Father, in the name of Jesus, I decree and declare that this is the day You have made, and I will rejoice and be glad in it, as written in Psalm 118:24. I dedicate this day to Your glory.

2. Lord, I declare that every detail of the wedding is aligned with Your perfect will, for Your Word says, 'The steps of a good man are ordered by the Lord, and He delights in his way' (Psalm 37:23). I trust You to guide every moment.

3. I decree that peace will reign over this day, for Your Word says, 'You will keep him in perfect peace, whose mind is stayed on You, because he trusts in You' (Isaiah 26:3). I declare that no anxiety will rob us of this joy.

4. Father, I rebuke every plan of the enemy to cause disruption or confusion. Your Word says, 'No weapon formed against you shall prosper, and every tongue which rises against you in judgment you shall condemn' (Isaiah 54:17). This day is covered by Your protection.

5. Lord, I declare that love and unity will prevail throughout the day, for Your Word says, 'Above all, love each other deeply, because love covers over a multitude of sins' (1 Peter 4:8, NIV). Let Your love overflow in every interaction.

6. In the name of Jesus, I decree that every person attending the wedding will be a source of blessing. Your Word says, 'Blessed is the man who walks not in the counsel of the wicked' (Psalm 1:1). I declare that all who come will be led by Your Spirit.

7. Father, I declare that the ceremony will reflect Your glory, for Your Word says, 'Whether you eat or drink or whatever you do, do it all for the glory of God' (1 Corinthians 10:31). May Your presence be evident in every moment.

8. Lord, I decree that the joy of the Lord will be my strength on this day, as written in Nehemiah 8:10. I rebuke every spirit of fatigue, stress, or discouragement.

9. Father, I declare that the covenant made today will be sealed by Your Spirit. Your Word says, 'Therefore what God has joined together, let no one separate' (Mark 10:9, NIV). This union is unbreakable in You.

10. In the name of Jesus, I decree that every logistical detail will flow smoothly. Your Word says, 'Let all things be done decently and in order' (1 Corinthians 14:40). I trust You to oversee every arrangement.

11. Lord, I declare that the weather will cooperate with Your plan, for Your Word says, 'He made the storm be still, and the waves of the sea were hushed' (Psalm 107:29, ESV). I speak peace over the atmosphere.

12. Father, I decree that the spirit of joy and celebration will fill the hearts of all present. Your Word says, 'Rejoice with those who rejoice' (Romans 12:15). I declare a spirit of unity and shared joy.

13. Lord, I declare that the vows exchanged will be spoken with sincerity and commitment, for Your Word says, 'When you make

a vow to God, do not delay to pay it; for He has no pleasure in fools. Pay what you have vowed' (Ecclesiastes 5:4). These promises are holy and binding.

14. In the name of Jesus, I decree that the presence of the Holy Spirit will fill the venue. Your Word says, 'For where two or three are gathered in My name, there am I with them' (Matthew 18:20). I invite You to dwell among us.

15. Father, I declare that the union formed today will be fruitful and blessed. Your Word says, 'God blessed them and said to them, "Be fruitful and increase in number; fill the earth and subdue it"' (Genesis 1:28). I speak blessings over this covenant.

16. Lord, I decree that gratitude will fill my heart and overflow in my speech, for Your Word says, 'Give thanks in all circumstances; for this is God's will for you in Christ Jesus' (1 Thessalonians 5:18). I give You praise for this day.

17. Father, I declare that every challenge or setback will be turned into a testimony of Your faithfulness. Your Word says, 'And we know that in all things God works for the good of those who love Him' (Romans 8:28). I trust You to work all things for good.

18. Lord, I decree that the celebration will be filled with laughter and joy, for Your Word says, 'A cheerful heart is good medicine' (Proverbs 17:22, NIV). Let this day bring healing and happiness to all who attend.

19. Father, I declare that the blessings of this day will extend into the marriage, for Your Word says, 'The blessing of the Lord

makes one rich, and He adds no sorrow with it' (Proverbs 10:22). This day is the start of a lifelong blessing.

20. In the name of Jesus, I decree that every moment of this day will glorify You. Your Word says, 'Let your light so shine before men, that they may see your good works and glorify your Father in heaven' (Matthew 5:16). May Your name be lifted high in every detail.

**Closing Prayer:**
Father, I thank You for this sacred day, a celebration of Your faithfulness and love. I pray that every moment reflects Your glory and that peace, joy, and unity prevail. Let this day mark the beginning of a covenant that honors You and stands as a testimony to Your goodness. Bless all who attend, and let Your presence guide every detail. In Jesus' name, Amen.

# CHAPTER 17

# Declarations for Groomsmen to Say Over the Groom

**Scripture Focus:**
*"As iron sharpens iron, so one person sharpens another."*
*Proverbs 27:17 (NIV)*

**Introduction:**
The role of a groomsman is more than ceremonial; it is a spiritual responsibility to pray for, support, and encourage the groom as he steps into a new season of his life. Proverbs 27:17 reminds us of the importance of sharpening one another through accountability, prayer, and encouragement.

These declarations empower the groomsmen to speak life over the groom, affirming his role as a godly husband, leader, and protector. Through these words, they stand as spiritual brothers, strengthening him for the covenant he is about to enter.

## 20 Declarations for Groomsmen to Say Over the Groom

1. Father, in the name of Jesus, we decree and declare that our brother will love his wife as Christ loves the Church, for Your Word says, 'Husbands, love your wives, just as Christ loved the church and gave Himself up for her' (Ephesians 5:25). He will lead with sacrificial love.

2. Lord, we declare that he will walk in wisdom as the head of his household, for Your Word says, 'The husband is the head of the wife as Christ is the head of the church' (Ephesians 5:23). He will lead with humility and grace.

3. We decree that his marriage will be established on the foundation of Christ, for Your Word says, 'Unless the Lord builds the house, the builders labor in vain' (Psalm 127:1). His union will stand firm in You.

4. Father, we declare that he will honor his wife in all things, for Your Word says, 'Husbands, likewise, dwell with them with understanding, giving honor to the wife' (1 Peter 3:7). He will treat her with respect and dignity.

5. Lord, we decree that he will guard his heart and remain faithful, for Your Word says, 'I have made a covenant with my eyes' (Job 31:1). He will remain pure in thought and deed.

6. We declare that he will walk in patience and understanding, for Your Word says, 'Love is patient, love is kind. It does not envy, it does not boast, it is not proud' (1 Corinthians 13:4). He will embody Your love in his marriage.

7. Father, we rebuke every plan of the enemy against his marriage. Your Word says, 'No weapon formed against you shall prosper' (Isaiah 54:17). His marriage is protected under Your blood.

8. Lord, we decree that he will be a provider for his family, for Your Word says, 'If anyone does not provide for his relatives, and especially for his own household, he has denied the faith' (1 Timothy 5:8). He will steward his resources with wisdom.

9. We declare that he will lead his family in prayer and worship, for Your Word says, 'As for me and my house, we will serve the Lord' (Joshua 24:15). His home will be a sanctuary of Your presence.

10. Father, we decree that he will be strong and courageous, for Your Word says, 'Be strong and courageous. Do not be afraid; do not be discouraged, for the Lord your God will be with you wherever you go' (Joshua 1:9). He will face every challenge with faith.

11. Lord, we declare that he will walk in humility, for Your Word says, 'Do nothing out of selfish ambition or vain conceit. Rather, in humility value others above yourselves' (Philippians 2:3, NIV). He will put his wife's needs above his own.

12. We decree that he will be quick to listen and slow to anger, for Your Word says, 'My dear brothers and sisters, take note of this: Everyone should be quick to listen, slow to speak, and slow to become angry' (James 1:19, NIV). He will foster peace in his home.

13. Father, we declare that he will remain steadfast in his faith, for Your Word says, 'Therefore, my beloved brethren, be steadfast, immovable, always abounding in the work of the Lord' (1 Corinthians 15:58). His life will be a testimony of Your faithfulness.

14. Lord, we decree that he will be a protector of his wife and family, for Your Word says, 'Be on your guard; stand firm in the faith; be courageous; be strong' (1 Corinthians 16:13, NIV). He will shield his family from harm.

15. We declare that his words will build up and not tear down, for Your Word says, 'Let no corrupt word proceed out of your mouth, but what is good for necessary edification' (Ephesians 4:29). He will speak life into his marriage.

16. Father, we decree that he will remain faithful in prayer, for Your Word says, 'Pray without ceasing' (1 Thessalonians 5:17). He will cover his marriage and family with prayer daily.

17. Lord, we declare that he will walk in forgiveness, for Your Word says, 'Forgive as the Lord forgave you' (Colossians 3:13, NIV). He will be quick to forgive and slow to hold grudges.

18. We decree that he will be a reflection of Christ's love, for Your Word says, 'And walk in the way of love, just as Christ loved us and gave Himself up for us as a fragrant offering and sacrifice to God' (Ephesians 5:2, NIV).

19. Father, we declare that his marriage will bear fruit for generations, for Your Word says, 'You will eat the fruit of your

labor; blessings and prosperity will be yours' (Psalm 128:2, NIV). His legacy will glorify You.

20. Lord, we decree that he will walk in unity with his wife, for Your Word says, 'Make every effort to keep the unity of the Spirit through the bond of peace' (Ephesians 4:3, NIV). Their union will remain unbreakable in You.

**Closing Prayer:**

Father, we lift up our brother in prayer, asking that You strengthen, guide, and bless him as he steps into the role of a husband. Cover him with wisdom, humility, and grace, and equip him to lead his family according to Your Word. May his marriage be a testimony of Your faithfulness and love. In Jesus' name, Amen.

# CHAPTER 18

# Declarations for Bridesmaids to Say Over the Bride

**Scripture Focus:**
*"She is clothed with strength and dignity;
she can laugh at the days to come."*
Proverbs 31:25 (NIV)

**Introduction:**

As bridesmaids, the role goes beyond standing by the bride on her wedding day—it is a spiritual duty to speak life, strength, and blessings over her. Proverbs 31:25 describes a woman who is clothed with strength and dignity, prepared to face the future with joy and confidence. Through prayer and declarations, bridesmaids can cover the bride in God's grace, peace, and protection as she steps into her new role as a wife.

These declarations will empower bridesmaids to pray over the bride, affirming her worth and preparing her heart for the covenant she is about to enter.

# 20 Declarations for Bridesmaids to Say Over the Bride

1. Father, in the name of Jesus, we decree and declare that our sister is clothed with strength and dignity, as Your Word says, 'She is clothed with strength and dignity; she can laugh at the days to come' (Proverbs 31:25). She walks in confidence and grace.

2. Lord, we declare that she will be a virtuous wife, for Your Word says, 'Who can find a virtuous wife? For her worth is far above rubies' (Proverbs 31:10). She is a treasure in Your sight and her husband's.

3. We decree that she will walk in wisdom and kindness, for Your Word says, 'She opens her mouth with wisdom, and on her tongue is the law of kindness' (Proverbs 31:26). She will speak life and encouragement.

4. Father, we declare that she is filled with peace on her wedding day, for Your Word says, 'You will keep him in perfect peace, whose mind is stayed on You, because he trusts in You' (Isaiah 26:3). She trusts in You completely.

5. Lord, we decree that her marriage will be fruitful and blessed, for Your Word says, 'God blessed them and said to them, "Be fruitful and increase in number"' (Genesis 1:28). Her union will bring forth joy and abundance.

6. We declare that she will walk in unity with her husband, for Your Word says, 'The two shall become one flesh. So they are

no longer two but one flesh' (Mark 10:8). Her marriage will reflect divine oneness.

7. Father, we decree that she will honor and respect her husband, for Your Word says, 'Let the wife see that she respects her husband' (Ephesians 5:33). She will be a source of encouragement and strength to him.

8. Lord, we declare that she will walk in humility and grace, for Your Word says, 'Do nothing out of selfish ambition or vain conceit. Rather, in humility value others above yourselves' (Philippians 2:3, NIV). She will reflect Your heart.

9. We decree that she will be a wise steward of her home, for Your Word says, 'The wise woman builds her house, but with her own hands the foolish one tears hers down' (Proverbs 14:1). She will build her home with wisdom.

10. Father, we declare that she will be a source of joy and peace, for Your Word says, 'A cheerful heart is good medicine' (Proverbs 17:22, NIV). Her presence will bring joy to her household.

11. Lord, we decree that she will walk in purity and holiness, for Your Word says, 'Blessed are the pure in heart, for they will see God' (Matthew 5:8). She will keep her heart aligned with You.

12. We declare that she will walk in faith, for Your Word says, 'Blessed is she who has believed that the Lord would fulfill His promises to her' (Luke 1:45, NIV). She stands firm on Your Word.

13. Father, we decree that she will forgive quickly and love deeply,

for Your Word says, 'Bear with each other and forgive one another... Forgive as the Lord forgave you' (Colossians 3:13, NIV). Her heart will remain tender.

14. Lord, we declare that she will remain faithful to You and her husband, for Your Word says, 'Let love and faithfulness never leave you; bind them around your neck, write them on the tablet of your heart' (Proverbs 3:3, NIV).

15. We decree that she will speak words that edify and uplift, for Your Word says, 'Let your conversation be always full of grace, seasoned with salt' (Colossians 4:6, NIV). Her words will bring life.

16. Father, we declare that she will honor her covenant, for Your Word says, 'When you make a vow to God, do not delay to fulfill it' (Ecclesiastes 5:4, NIV). She will keep her vows with reverence.

17. Lord, we decree that her marriage will be a testimony of Your faithfulness, for Your Word says, 'Let your light so shine before men, that they may see your good works and glorify your Father in heaven' (Matthew 5:16).

18. We declare that she will be a source of strength and encouragement, for Your Word says, 'Therefore encourage one another and build each other up' (1 Thessalonians 5:11, NIV). She will lift up her husband and those around her.

19. Father, we decree that her home will be a sanctuary of peace and love, for Your Word says, 'The Lord bless you and keep you;

the Lord make His face shine on you and be gracious to you' (Numbers 6:24-25).

20. Lord, we declare that her future is bright, for Your Word says, 'For I know the plans I have for you, declares the Lord, plans for welfare and not for evil, to give you a future and a hope' (Jeremiah 29:11, ESV). She will walk confidently into her new season.

**Closing Prayer:**
Father, we thank You for our sister, who is about to enter a new season of her life. We ask that You bless her abundantly, guide her steps, and fill her with Your Spirit. May her marriage glorify You, and may her life be a testimony of Your love and faithfulness. Surround her with peace and joy on this day and forevermore. In Jesus' name, Amen.

# CHAPTER 19

## Declarations for Mothers to Say Over Their Sons on the Wedding Day

*Scripture Focus:*
*"The father of the righteous will greatly rejoice, and he who begets a wise child will delight in him."*
*Proverbs 23:24 (NKJV)*

**Introduction:**

A mother's blessing carries profound spiritual weight. On her son's wedding day, she stands as a witness to his new covenant, offering prayers and declarations that will shape his journey as a husband. Proverbs 23:24 highlights the joy and pride of a parent whose child walks in righteousness.

These declarations equip mothers to speak blessings over their sons, affirming their roles as godly men, faithful husbands, and wise leaders. They release him into his new season with love, faith, and confidence in God's promises.

## 20 Declarations for Mothers to Say Over Their Sons on the Wedding Day

1. Father, in the name of Jesus, I decree and declare that my son is a man of righteousness, for Your Word says, 'The steps of a good man are ordered by the Lord' (Psalm 37:23). I release him into this new season with confidence in Your guidance.

2. Lord, I declare that my son will love his wife as Christ loves the Church, for Your Word says, 'Husbands, love your wives, just as Christ also loved the church and gave Himself for her' (Ephesians 5:25). He will lead with sacrificial love.

3. I decree that my son will walk in wisdom as a husband, for Your Word says, 'Wisdom is the principal thing; therefore get wisdom. And in all your getting, get understanding' (Proverbs 4:7). He will lead his household with wisdom and discernment.

4. Father, I declare that my son will honor the covenant he makes today, for Your Word says, 'When you make a vow to God, do not delay to fulfill it' (Ecclesiastes 5:4). He will remain faithful to his promises.

5. Lord, I decree that my son will protect and cherish his wife, for Your Word says, 'He who finds a wife finds a good thing and obtains favor from the Lord' (Proverbs 18:22). He will recognize and honor the gift You have given him.

6. I declare that my son's marriage will be fruitful, for Your Word says, 'God blessed them and said to them, "Be fruitful and multiply"' (Genesis 1:28). His union will bring forth blessings and legacy.

7. Father, I decree that my son will walk in humility, for Your Word says, 'Do nothing out of selfish ambition or vain conceit. Rather, in humility value others above yourselves' (Philippians 2:3, NIV). He will put his wife's needs above his own.

8. Lord, I declare that my son will lead his home in prayer and worship, for Your Word says, 'As for me and my house, we will serve the Lord' (Joshua 24:15). His home will be a sanctuary of Your presence.

9. I decree that my son will remain faithful in every aspect of his life, for Your Word says, 'A faithful man will abound with blessings' (Proverbs 28:20). He will honor his covenant with unwavering faithfulness.

10. Father, I declare that my son will guard his heart and mind, for Your Word says, 'Above all else, guard your heart, for everything you do flows from it' (Proverbs 4:23). He will walk in purity and holiness.

11. Lord, I decree that my son will communicate with love and kindness, for Your Word says, 'Let your speech always be with grace, seasoned with salt, that you may know how you ought to answer each one' (Colossians 4:6). His words will build and not tear down.

12. I declare that my son will be a peacemaker in his home, for Your Word says, 'Blessed are the peacemakers, for they shall be called sons of God' (Matthew 5:9). He will cultivate an atmosphere of peace and harmony.

13. Father, I decree that my son will rely on Your strength, for Your Word says, 'I can do all things through Christ who strengthens me' (Philippians 4:13). He will overcome every challenge with Your help.

14. Lord, I declare that my son's marriage will glorify You, for Your Word says, 'Whatever you do, do it all for the glory of God' (1 Corinthians 10:31). His union will be a testimony of Your faithfulness.

15. I decree that my son will honor his wife, for Your Word says, 'Husbands, likewise, dwell with them with understanding, giving honor to the wife' (1 Peter 3:7). He will treat her with respect and love.

16. Father, I declare that my son's home will be built on a firm foundation, for Your Word says, 'Unless the Lord builds the house, they labor in vain who build it' (Psalm 127:1). His marriage will stand strong in You.

17. Lord, I decree that my son will be patient and kind, for Your Word says, 'Love is patient, love is kind. It does not envy, it does not boast, it is not proud' (1 Corinthians 13:4). He will walk in love daily.

18. I declare that my son will be a godly father in the future, for Your Word says, 'Fathers, do not provoke your children to anger, but bring them up in the discipline and instruction of the Lord' (Ephesians 6:4). He will lead his family with love and wisdom.

19. Father, I decree that my son will always seek Your guidance, for Your Word says, 'Trust in the Lord with all your heart and lean not on your own understanding' (Proverbs 3:5). He will acknowledge You in all his ways.

20. Lord, I declare that my son will fulfill the purpose You have for him, for Your Word says, 'For I know the plans I have for you, declares the Lord, plans to prosper you and not to harm you' (Jeremiah 29:11). His marriage will align with Your divine purpose.

**Closing Prayer:**
Father, I thank You for the gift of my son and for this sacred day. I bless him as he steps into the role of a husband, asking that You guide, strengthen, and protect him. May his marriage reflect Your love, and may he walk in wisdom, humility, and faithfulness. Let this covenant glorify You and serve as a testimony of Your grace. In Jesus' name, Amen.

# CHAPTER 20

# Declarations for Mothers to Say Over Their Daughters on the Wedding Day

**Scripture Focus:**
*"Her children rise up and call her blessed;
her husband also, and he praises her."*
*Proverbs 31:28 (NKJV)*

**Introduction:**

A mother's words over her daughter on her wedding day carry a profound blessing that sets the tone for her marriage. Proverbs 31:28 speaks of the honor bestowed on a woman of virtue, a woman whose life reflects God's goodness. As a mother, you have the privilege to speak prophetic blessings over your daughter, affirming her worth, equipping her for marriage, and entrusting her future to the Lord.

These declarations are designed to empower mothers to release their daughters into their new season with faith, love, and encouragement.

## 20 Declarations for Mothers to Say Over Their Daughters on the Wedding Day

1. Father, in the name of Jesus, I decree and declare that my daughter is a virtuous woman, for Your Word says, 'Her worth is far above rubies' (Proverbs 31:10). She is a treasure to her husband and all who know her.

2. Lord, I declare that she will walk in strength and dignity, for Your Word says, 'She is clothed with strength and dignity; she can laugh at the days to come' (Proverbs 31:25). She will face her future with confidence.

3. I decree that my daughter's marriage will be rooted in love, for Your Word says, 'Above all, love each other deeply, because love covers over a multitude of sins' (1 Peter 4:8, NIV). Her home will overflow with love and forgiveness.

4. Father, I declare that my daughter will be a wise and kind wife, for Your Word says, 'She opens her mouth with wisdom, and on her tongue is the law of
kindness' (Proverbs 31:26). Her words will build and encourage.

5. Lord, I decree that my daughter's marriage will be fruitful and blessed, for Your Word says, 'God blessed them and said to them, "Be fruitful and multiply"' (Genesis 1:28). Her union will bring forth joy and legacy.

6. I declare that my daughter will honor her husband, for Your Word says, 'Let the wife see that she respects her husband' (Ephesians 5:33). She will uplift and encourage him in all things.

7. Father, I decree that my daughter will manage her household with wisdom, for Your Word says, 'The wise woman builds her house, but with her own hands the foolish one tears hers down' (Proverbs 14:1). She will create a home of peace and harmony.

8. Lord, I declare that she will remain faithful and steadfast, for Your Word says, 'Let love and faithfulness never leave you; bind them around your neck, write them on the tablet of your heart' (Proverbs 3:3, NIV). Her commitment will be unwavering.

9. I decree that my daughter will walk in humility and grace, for Your Word says, 'Do nothing out of selfish ambition or vain conceit. Rather, in humility value others above yourselves' (Philippians 2:3, NIV). She will reflect Your heart in all she does.

10. Father, I declare that her marriage will glorify You, for Your Word says, 'Whatever you do, do it all for the glory of God' (1 Corinthians 10:31). Her union will be a testimony of Your faithfulness.

11. Lord, I decree that my daughter will walk in unity with her husband, for Your Word says, 'The two will become one flesh' (Ephesians 5:31). Their bond will be unbreakable.

12. I declare that my daughter will trust in Your guidance, for Your Word says, 'Trust in the Lord with all your heart and lean not on your own understanding' (Proverbs 3:5). She will seek You in every decision.

13. Father, I decree that my daughter will create a home filled with Your presence, for Your Word says, 'As for me and my house,

we will serve the Lord' (Joshua 24:15). Her household will honor You.

14. Lord, I declare that my daughter will remain steadfast in faith, for Your Word says, 'Be steadfast, immovable, always abounding in the work of the Lord' (1 Corinthians 15:58). Her life will reflect unwavering faith.

15. I decree that my daughter will walk in peace, for Your Word says, 'The peace of God, which transcends all understanding, will guard your hearts and your minds in Christ Jesus' (Philippians 4:7). Her heart will be guarded by Your peace.

16. Father, I declare that she will be a godly example to her children, for Your Word says, 'Train up a child in the way he should go, and when he is old he will not depart from it' (Proverbs 22:6). She will nurture her family in Your ways.

17. Lord, I decree that her marriage will withstand every trial, for Your Word says, 'Though one may be overpowered, two can defend themselves. A cord of three strands is not quickly broken' (Ecclesiastes 4:12). You are the third strand in her union.

18. I declare that my daughter will walk in forgiveness, for Your Word says, 'Bear with each other and forgive one another... Forgive as the Lord forgave you' (Colossians 3:13, NIV). She will extend grace to her husband and others.

19. Father, I decree that her marriage will be protected from every attack of the enemy, for Your Word says, 'No weapon formed

against you shall prosper' (Isaiah 54:17). Her home is covered by Your protection.

20. Lord, I declare that my daughter will shine brightly, for Your Word says, 'Let your light so shine before men, that they may see your good works and glorify your Father in heaven' (Matthew 5:16). Her life and marriage will reflect Your glory.

**Closing Prayer:**
Father, I thank You for my daughter and for this sacred day. I release her into Your care as she steps into the role of a wife. Bless her marriage with love, unity, and faithfulness. May her life be a reflection of Your goodness, and may her union glorify You in all things. Surround her with peace and joy, and let her walk confidently into this new season. In Jesus' name, Amen.

# SECTION 3

## BECOMING THE RIGHT PARTNER

# CHAPTER 21

# Declarations for Fathers to Say Over Their Sons on the Wedding Day

**Scripture Focus:**
"Train up a child in the way he should go,
and when he is old, he will not depart from it."
Proverbs 22:6 (NKJV)

**Introduction:**

A father's blessing over his son on his wedding day is a powerful affirmation of his role as a man of God, a loving husband, and a faithful leader. Proverbs 22:6 reminds us of the enduring impact of a father's guidance. This day marks a new chapter for the son, and the father's words serve as both a release and a covering for the journey ahead.

These declarations enable fathers to speak life, strength, and wisdom into their sons as they step into the sacred covenant of marriage.

## 20 Declarations for Fathers to Say Over Their Sons on the Wedding Day

1. Father, in the name of Jesus, I decree and declare that my son is a man of integrity and honor, for Your Word says, 'The righteous man walks in his integrity; his children are blessed after him' (Proverbs 20:7). He will lead his family with righteousness.

2. Lord, I declare that my son will love his wife with the selfless love of Christ, for Your Word says, 'Husbands, love your wives, just as Christ loved the church and gave Himself up for her' (Ephesians 5:25). He will love sacrificially.

3. I decree that my son's steps are ordered by the Lord, for Your Word says, 'The steps of a good man are ordered by the Lord, and He delights in his way' (Psalm 37:23). He will walk in Your guidance and wisdom.

4. Father, I declare that my son will honor his covenant, for Your Word says, 'When you make a vow to God, do not delay to fulfill it' (Ecclesiastes 5:4). He will remain steadfast in his promises.

5. Lord, I decree that my son will be a protector and provider, for Your Word says, 'If anyone does not provide for his relatives, and especially for his own household, he has denied the faith' (1 Timothy 5:8). He will faithfully care for his family.

6. I declare that my son will remain faithful in all aspects of his marriage, for Your Word says, 'A faithful man will abound with blessings' (Proverbs 28:20). He will honor his wife with loyalty and devotion.

7. Father, I decree that my son will lead his home with humility and strength, for Your Word says, 'Be strong and courageous. Do not be afraid; do not be discouraged, for the Lord your God will be with you wherever you go' (Joshua 1:9). He will walk confidently in Your presence.

8. Lord, I declare that my son will model Christlike leadership, for Your Word says, 'For even the Son of Man did not come to be served, but to serve' (Mark 10:45). He will lead his family with a servant's heart.

9. I decree that my son will walk in wisdom, for Your Word says, 'If any of you lacks wisdom, you should ask God, who gives generously to all without finding fault, and it will be given to you' (James 1:5). He will seek Your counsel in every decision.

10. Father, I declare that my son will guard his heart and mind, for Your Word says, 'Above all else, guard your heart, for everything you do flows from it' (Proverbs 4:23). He will walk in purity and discernment.

11. Lord, I decree that my son will create a home of peace and love, for Your Word says, 'Blessed are the peacemakers, for they shall be called sons of God' (Matthew 5:9). His household will reflect Your peace.

12. I declare that my son will rely on Your strength, for Your Word says, 'I can do all things through Christ who strengthens me' (Philippians 4:13). He will overcome every challenge with Your help.

13. Father, I decree that my son's marriage will be fruitful, for Your Word says, 'God blessed them and said, "Be fruitful and multiply"' (Genesis 1:28). His union will bring forth blessings and legacy.

14. Lord, I declare that my son will honor his wife in every way, for Your Word says, 'Husbands, likewise, dwell with them with understanding, giving honor to the wife' (1 Peter 3:7). He will be a source of strength and encouragement to her.

15. I decree that my son will remain steadfast in his faith, for Your Word says, 'Be steadfast, immovable, always abounding in the work of the Lord' (1 Corinthians 15:58). His life will glorify You.

16. Father, I declare that my son will build a home that honors You, for Your Word says, 'Unless the Lord builds the house, the builders labor in vain' (Psalm 127:1). His marriage will stand firm in Your purpose.

17. Lord, I decree that my son will communicate with love and understanding, for Your Word says, 'Let your conversation be always full of grace, seasoned with salt' (Colossians 4:6). His words will edify and strengthen.

18. I declare that my son will remain a godly example to future generations, for Your Word says, 'The righteous man walks in his integrity; his children are blessed after him' (Proverbs 20:7). He will leave a lasting legacy.

19. Father, I decree that my son's marriage will be protected from the schemes of the enemy, for Your Word says, 'No weapon

formed against you shall prosper' (Isaiah 54:17). His home is covered under Your protection.

20. Lord, I declare that my son will walk in unity with his wife, for Your Word says, 'Can two walk together, unless they are agreed?' (Amos 3:3). Their union will remain strong and united in You.

**Closing Prayer:**
Father, I thank You for my son and for this sacred day. I release him into this new chapter of his life with faith and confidence in Your plan. Bless his marriage, guide his steps, and strengthen him to be a godly husband and leader. Let his life reflect Your glory and faithfulness. In Jesus' name, Amen.

# CHAPTER 22

# Declarations for Fathers to Say Over Their Daughters on the Wedding Day

**Scripture Focus:**
*"I will walk among you and be your God, and you will be My people."*
*Leviticus 26:12 (NIV)*

**Introduction:**
A father's words over his daughter on her wedding day signify his blessing and release as she enters a new season of life. This moment is an opportunity to affirm her worth, speak God's promises, and entrust her future to His hands. The father's blessing carries spiritual authority, fortifying her marriage and reinforcing her identity in Christ.

These declarations guide fathers to bless their daughters with confidence, love, and faith, covering them with God's Word and releasing them into their covenant relationship.

## 20 Declarations for Fathers to Say Over Their Daughters on the Wedding Day

1. Father, in the name of Jesus, I decree and declare that my daughter is blessed and highly favored, for Your Word says, 'You are a chosen people, a royal priesthood, a holy nation, God's special possession' (1 Peter 2:9, NIV). She is precious in Your sight.

2. Lord, I declare that my daughter will walk in strength and dignity, for Your Word says, 'She is clothed with strength and dignity; she can laugh at the days to come' (Proverbs 31:25). She will face her future with courage and joy.

3. I decree that her marriage will be fruitful and blessed, for Your Word says, 'God blessed them and said to them, "Be fruitful and increase in number; fill the earth and subdue it"' (Genesis 1:28). Her union will bring forth blessings and legacy.

4. Father, I declare that my daughter will honor her covenant, for Your Word says, 'When you make a vow to God, do not delay to fulfill it' (Ecclesiastes 5:4). She will remain faithful to her promises.

5. Lord, I decree that my daughter will walk in unity with her husband, for Your Word says, 'The two will become one flesh. So they are no longer two, but one flesh' (Mark 10:8). Their bond will be unbreakable.

6. I declare that my daughter will create a home filled with Your

presence, for Your Word says, 'As for me and my house, we will serve the Lord' (Joshua 24:15). Her household will glorify You.

7. Father, I decree that my daughter will honor and respect her husband, for Your Word says, 'Let the wife see that she respects her husband' (Ephesians 5:33). She will uplift and encourage him in all things.

8. Lord, I declare that my daughter will be filled with wisdom and grace, for Your Word says, 'She opens her mouth with wisdom, and the teaching of kindness is on her tongue' (Proverbs 31:26). She will speak life and truth in all she does.

9. I decree that my daughter will walk in purity, for Your Word says, 'Blessed are the pure in heart, for they shall see God' (Matthew 5:8). Her life will reflect Your holiness.

10. Father, I declare that my daughter will remain steadfast in faith, for Your Word says, 'Be steadfast, immovable, always abounding in the work of the Lord' (1 Corinthians 15:58). Her life will glorify You.

11. Lord, I decree that my daughter will rely on Your strength, for Your Word says, 'I can do all things through Christ who strengthens me' (Philippians 4:13). She will overcome every challenge with Your help.

12. I declare that my daughter will walk in peace, for Your Word says, 'The peace of God, which transcends all understanding, will guard your hearts and your minds in Christ Jesus' (Philippians 4:7). Her heart will be guarded by Your peace.

13. Father, I decree that my daughter will be a wise steward of her home, for Your Word says, 'The wise woman builds her house, but with her own hands the foolish one tears hers down' (Proverbs 14:1). She will build her home with wisdom.

14. Lord, I declare that my daughter's marriage will be protected from every attack of the enemy, for Your Word says, 'No weapon formed against you shall
prosper' (Isaiah 54:17). Her union is covered by Your protection.

15. I decree that my daughter will be a reflection of Your love, for Your Word says, 'Walk in the way of love, just as Christ loved us and gave Himself up for us as a fragrant offering and sacrifice to God' (Ephesians 5:2, NIV).

16. Father, I declare that my daughter will be a source of joy and encouragement, for Your Word says, 'A cheerful heart is good medicine' (Proverbs 17:22, NIV). Her presence will uplift her husband and family.

17. Lord, I decree that my daughter will forgive quickly and love deeply, for Your Word says, 'Bear with each other and forgive one another... Forgive as the Lord forgave you' (Colossians 3:13, NIV). She will walk in grace and mercy.

18. I declare that my daughter will seek Your guidance in every decision, for Your Word says, 'Trust in the Lord with all your heart and lean not on your own understanding' (Proverbs 3:5). She will acknowledge You in all her ways.

19. Father, I decree that my daughter's future is secure in Your hands, for Your Word says, 'For I know the plans I have for you, declares the Lord, plans to prosper you and not to harm you' (Jeremiah 29:11). She will walk confidently in Your purpose.

20. Lord, I declare that my daughter will shine brightly, for Your Word says, 'Let your light so shine before men, that they may see your good works and glorify your Father in heaven' (Matthew 5:16). Her life and marriage will reflect Your glory.

**Closing Prayer:**
Father, I thank You for the gift of my daughter. On this sacred day, I release her into this new chapter of life with faith in Your plan. Bless her marriage, guide her steps, and surround her with Your love and protection. May her union reflect Your glory and bring joy to all who witness it. In Jesus' name, Amen.

# CHAPTER 23

# Declarations Over Your Son for Their Spouse

**Scripture Focus:**
*"He who finds a wife finds a good thing and obtains favor from the Lord."*
*Proverbs 18:22 (NKJV)*

**Introduction:**
A parent's prayer over their son's future spouse is a seed of faith and an act of intercession. Proverbs 18:22 reminds us that finding a godly wife is a blessing and a sign of favor from the Lord. By declaring God's promises, parents can help pave the way for their son to walk in alignment with God's will, ensuring his spouse is a partner in purpose, faith, and destiny.

These declarations focus on praying for a spouse who complements, supports, and uplifts your son as they journey through life together.

## 20 Declarations Over Your Son for Their Spouse

1. Father, in the name of Jesus, I decree and declare that my son will find a wife who is a good thing and a sign of Your favor, for Your Word says, 'He who finds a wife finds a good thing and obtains favor from the Lord' (Proverbs 18:22). She will be a blessing in his life.

2. Lord, I declare that my son's future wife will be a woman of virtue and strength, for Your Word says, 'Who can find a virtuous wife? For her worth is far above
rubies' (Proverbs 31:10). She will be a treasure beyond measure.

3. I decree that my son will marry a woman who fears You, for Your Word says, 'Charm is deceptive, and beauty is fleeting; but a woman who fears the Lord is to be praised' (Proverbs 31:30, NIV). Her heart will be rooted in reverence for You.

4. Father, I declare that my son's wife will be a woman of wisdom and discernment, for Your Word says, 'She opens her mouth with wisdom, and the teaching of kindness is on her tongue' (Proverbs 31:26). She will speak life and truth.

5. Lord, I decree that my son will be yoked with a godly woman, for Your Word says, 'Do not be unequally yoked with unbelievers' (2 Corinthians 6:14). Their union will be rooted in shared faith.

6. I declare that my son's wife will be a woman of prayer, for Your Word says, 'The effective, fervent prayer of a righteous person avails much' (James 5:16). She will intercede for her family with power.

7. Father, I decree that my son's future wife will be a woman of peace, for Your Word says, 'Blessed are the peacemakers, for they shall be called sons of God' (Matthew 5:9). Her presence will bring harmony to their home.

8. Lord, I declare that my son's wife will be diligent and hardworking, for Your Word says, 'She watches over the affairs of her household and does not eat the bread of idleness' (Proverbs 31:27). She will steward her responsibilities with excellence.

9. I decree that my son's wife will love and respect him, for Your Word says, 'Let the wife see that she respects her husband' (Ephesians 5:33). Their marriage will be marked by mutual honor.

10. Father, I declare that my son's wife will be a partner in his purpose, for Your Word says, 'Two are better than one, because they have a good return for their labor' (Ecclesiastes 4:9). Together, they will fulfill their God-given destiny.

11. Lord, I decree that my son's wife will be kind and compassionate, for Your Word says, 'Be kind and compassionate to one another, forgiving each other, just as in Christ God forgave you' (Ephesians 4:32). She will reflect Your heart.

12. I declare that my son's wife will be a woman of strength and endurance, for Your Word says, 'She girds herself with strength, and strengthens her arms' (Proverbs 31:17). She will face life's challenges with courage.

13. Father, I decree that my son's wife will be a woman of faith, for Your Word says, 'Blessed is she who has believed that the Lord would fulfill His promises to her' (Luke 1:45, NIV). Her trust in You will never waver.

14. Lord, I declare that my son's wife will be a nurturing and loving mother, for Your Word says, 'Her children rise up and call her blessed' (Proverbs 31:28). She will raise their children in Your ways.

15. I decree that my son's wife will walk in purity and holiness, for Your Word says, 'Blessed are the pure in heart, for they will see God' (Matthew 5:8). Her life will be pleasing to You.

16. Father, I declare that my son's wife will have a heart of service, for Your Word says, 'Serve one another humbly in love' (Galatians 5:13). She will serve her family and others with joy.

17. Lord, I decree that my son's wife will support him in prayer and purpose, for Your Word says, 'A wife of noble character is her husband's crown' (Proverbs 12:4, NIV). She will be his greatest encourager.

18. I declare that my son's wife will walk in humility and grace, for Your Word says, 'Do nothing out of selfish ambition or vain conceit. Rather, in humility value others above yourselves' (Philippians 2:3, NIV). She will reflect Christ's character.

19. Father, I decree that my son's wife will be a blessing to all who know her, for Your Word says, 'The righteous are a tree of life,

and the one who is wise saves lives' (Proverbs 11:30, NIV). She will bring life and wisdom to her relationships.

20. Lord, I declare that my son's wife will be anointed and appointed by You, for Your Word says, 'For we are God's handiwork, created in Christ Jesus to do good works, which God prepared in advance for us to do' (Ephesians 2:10). Their union will fulfill Your divine purpose.

**Closing Prayer:**
Father, I thank You for the wife You have chosen for my son. I pray that You prepare her heart and mind for the covenant they will enter. Bless her with wisdom, strength, and grace. May their union glorify You and serve as a testimony of Your faithfulness. Surround them with Your love and protection, and let them walk boldly in the purpose You have for them. In Jesus' name, Amen.

# CHAPTER 24

# Declarations Over Your Daughter for Their Spouse

**Scripture Focus:**
*"The heart of her husband trusts in her, and he will have no lack of gain."*
*Proverbs 31:11 (ESV)*

**Introduction:**
A parent's prayer over their daughter's future spouse is a declaration of faith that God will bring a partner who honors, cherishes, and complements her. Proverbs 31:11 describes the trust and security a husband should have in his wife, reflecting a union rooted in mutual respect and Godly principles. Through these declarations, parents can intercede for a spouse who aligns with their daughter's purpose and destiny.

**20 Declarations Over Your Daughter for Their Spouse**

1. Father, in the name of Jesus, I decree and declare that my daughter's husband will be a man after Your own heart, for Your Word says, 'The Lord has sought out a man after His own heart' (1 Samuel 13:14). He will prioritize Your will above all else.

2. Lord, I declare that her husband will love her as Christ loves the Church, for Your Word says, 'Husbands, love your wives, just as Christ also loved the church and gave Himself for her' (Ephesians 5:25). His love will be selfless and enduring.

3. I decree that my daughter's husband will walk in integrity, for Your Word says, 'The righteous man walks in his integrity; his children are blessed after
him' (Proverbs 20:7). He will lead his family with honor.

4. Father, I declare that her husband will be a man of wisdom, for Your Word says, 'Blessed is the one who finds wisdom, and the one who gets understanding' (Proverbs 3:13). He will guide their home with discernment.

5. Lord, I decree that her husband will be a protector and provider, for Your Word says, 'But if anyone does not provide for his relatives, and especially for members of his household, he has denied the faith' (1 Timothy 5:8). He will care for his family with diligence.

6. I declare that her husband will be faithful and trustworthy, for Your Word says, 'A faithful man will abound with blessings' (Proverbs 28:20). His loyalty will never waver.

7. Father, I decree that her husband will be a man of prayer, for Your Word says, 'The effective, fervent prayer of a righteous man avails much' (James 5:16). He will cover his family in intercession.

8. Lord, I declare that her husband will walk in humility, for Your Word says, 'God opposes the proud but shows favor to the humble' (James 4:6). He will lead with a servant's heart.

9. I decree that her husband will honor her in every way, for Your Word says, 'Husbands, likewise, dwell with them with understanding, giving honor to the wife' (1 Peter 3:7). He will treat her with respect and tenderness.

10. Father, I declare that her husband will walk in unity with her, for Your Word says, 'The two shall become one flesh' (Mark 10:8). Their bond will reflect divine oneness.

11. Lord, I decree that her husband will encourage her in her calling, for Your Word says, 'And let us consider how we may spur one another on toward love and good deeds' (Hebrews 10:24). He will support her purpose and destiny.

12. I declare that her husband will be a godly father, for Your Word says, 'Fathers, do not provoke your children to anger, but bring them up in the discipline and instruction of the Lord' (Ephesians 6:4). He will nurture their children in Your ways.

13. Father, I decree that her husband will remain steadfast in faith, for Your Word says, 'Be on your guard; stand firm in the faith; be courageous; be strong' (1 Corinthians 16:13). His life will be a testimony of Your faithfulness.

14. Lord, I declare that her husband will be slow to anger and quick to listen, for Your Word says, 'Everyone should be quick to listen, slow to speak and slow to become angry' (James 1:19). He will foster peace in their home.

15. I decree that her husband will be a man of vision and purpose, for Your Word says, 'Where there is no vision, the people perish' (Proverbs 29:18). He will lead their family with divine direction.

16. Father, I declare that her husband will walk in purity, for Your Word says, 'How can a young man keep his way pure? By living according to Your word' (Psalm 119:9). His heart will remain devoted to You.

17. Lord, I decree that her husband will seek Your guidance in every decision, for Your Word says, 'Trust in the Lord with all your heart and lean not on your own understanding' (Proverbs 3:5). He will acknowledge You in all his ways.

18. I declare that her husband will walk in joy and peace, for Your Word says, 'The joy of the Lord is your strength' (Nehemiah 8:10) and 'The peace of God... will guard your hearts and minds' (Philippians 4:7). Their home will be filled with gladness.

19. Father, I decree that her husband will be a peacemaker, for Your Word says, 'Blessed are the peacemakers, for they will be called children of God' (Matthew 5:9). He will cultivate harmony in their family.

20. Lord, I declare that her husband will honor the covenant of

marriage, for Your Word says, 'Therefore what God has joined together, let no one separate' (Matthew 19:6). He will remain committed for life.

**Closing Prayer:**

Father, I thank You for the husband You are preparing for my daughter. May he walk in righteousness, wisdom, and faith, aligning with Your perfect will. Bless their union with peace, love, and joy, and let their lives together glorify You. Surround him with Your protection, and lead him in all his ways. In Jesus' name, Amen.

# CHAPTER 25

# Declarations That Break Marital Delay

**Scripture Focus:**
*"The vision is yet for an appointed time; but at the end it will speak, and it will not lie. Though it tarries, wait for it; be cause it will surely come, it will not tarry."*
*Habakkuk 2:3 (NKJV)*

**Introduction:**
Marital delay can be a source of deep frustration and discouragement, but the promises of God remind us that His timing is perfect. Habakkuk 2:3 encourages believers to trust in the appointed time for every vision and promise. This chapter equips you with declarations to confront and dismantle spiritual and emotional barriers to marriage while standing firmly on God's Word.

These declarations will release faith, uproot generational patterns, and break every form of delay that hinders God's timing for marriage.

## 20 Declarations That Break Marital Delay

1. Father, in the name of Jesus, I decree and declare that every spirit of delay over my life is broken, for Your Word says, 'For the vision is yet for an appointed time... though it tarries, wait for it; because it will surely come' (Habakkuk 2:3). My marriage will manifest in Your perfect timing.

2. Lord, I rebuke every generational curse or pattern of marital delay in my family line, for Your Word says, 'Christ redeemed us from the curse of the law by becoming a curse for us' (Galatians 3:13). I am set free through the blood of Jesus.

3. I decree that I will no longer be overlooked or hidden, for Your Word says, 'You are the light of the world. A city that is set on a hill cannot be hidden' (Matthew 5:14). I declare divine visibility over my life.

4. Father, I declare that I am prepared and ready for marriage, for Your Word says, 'He who finds a wife finds a good thing and obtains favor from the Lord' (Proverbs 18:22). I align myself with Your purpose for this season.

5. Lord, I decree that every demonic obstacle preventing my marital breakthrough is removed, for Your Word says, 'What is impossible with man is possible with God' (Luke 18:27). Nothing can hinder Your will for my life.

6. I declare that I am healed from past hurts and disappointments, for Your Word says, 'He heals the

brokenhearted and binds up their wounds' (Psalm 147:3). I step into marriage free of emotional baggage.

7. Father, I decree that my faith will not waver, for Your Word says, 'Let us hold fast the confession of our hope without wavering, for He who promised is
faithful' (Hebrews 10:23). I trust in Your promises.

8. Lord, I rebuke the spirit of fear concerning marriage, for Your Word says, 'For God has not given us a spirit of fear, but of power and of love and of a sound mind' (2 Timothy 1:7). I step into this season with boldness.

9. I declare that I will not be anxious about finding a spouse, for Your Word says, 'Do not be anxious about anything, but in every situation, by prayer and petition, with thanksgiving, present your requests to God' (Philippians 4:6). I rest in Your provision.

10. Father, I decree that I am surrounded by godly counsel and wisdom, for Your Word says, 'Plans fail for lack of counsel, but with many advisers they succeed' (Proverbs 15:22). I receive divine guidance in this season.

11. Lord, I declare that every delay caused by distractions is broken, for Your Word says, 'Set your minds on things above, not on earthly things' (Colossians 3:2). My focus is on You and Your plans for my life.

12. I decree that my marriage will glorify You, for Your Word says, 'So whether you eat or drink or whatever you do, do it all for the glory of God' (1 Corinthians 10:31). My union will reflect Your purpose.

13. Father, I declare that every spirit of rejection is uprooted, for Your Word says, 'The stone the builders rejected has become the cornerstone' (Psalm 118:22). I am chosen and accepted by You.

14. Lord, I decree that I am stepping into the fullness of Your blessings, for Your Word says, 'The blessing of the Lord makes rich, and He adds no sorrow with it' (Proverbs 10:22). My marriage will be a blessing without sorrow.

15. I declare that I will walk in purity and holiness as I prepare for marriage, for Your Word says, 'Blessed are the pure in heart, for they shall see God' (Matthew 5:8). I consecrate myself to You.

16. Father, I decree that my heart is open to Your timing and direction, for Your Word says, 'Trust in the Lord with all your heart and lean not on your own understanding' (Proverbs 3:5). I surrender my timeline to You.

17. Lord, I rebuke every lie of the enemy that says I will never marry, for Your Word says, 'You shall know the truth, and the truth shall make you free' (John 8:32). I stand on the truth of Your promises.

18. I declare that I will discern the right spouse, for Your Word says, 'And this I pray, that your love may abound still more and more in knowledge and all discernment' (Philippians 1:9). I will choose wisely under Your guidance.

19. Father, I decree that my marriage will come in Your perfect season, for Your Word says, 'He has made everything beautiful in its time' (Ecclesiastes 3:11). I trust in Your perfect timing.

20. Lord, I declare that I am free from every spirit of delay, for Your Word says, 'If the Son sets you free, you will be free indeed' (John 8:36). I walk in the freedom and fulfillment of Your promises.

**Closing Prayer:**

Father, I thank You for breaking every chain of marital delay over my life. I trust in Your perfect timing and align myself with Your will. Remove every obstacle and distraction, and prepare me for the union You have ordained. May my marriage reflect Your glory and bring joy to all who witness it. In Jesus' name, Amen.

# CHAPTER 26

# Declarations to find a Godly Man

***Scripture Focus:***
*"Delight yourself also in the Lord, and
He shall give you the desires of your heart."
Psalm 37:4 (NKJV)*

**Introduction:**
Finding a godly man is not about chance but about alignment with God's purpose and principles. Psalm 37:4 teaches us that delighting in the Lord aligns our desires with His will. This chapter equips you with declarations that position your heart, mind, and spirit to recognize and attract the man God has prepared for you.

These declarations will align your desires with God's, guide your choices, and rebuke distractions and counterfeits.

## 20 Declarations to Find a Godly Man

1. Father, in the name of Jesus, I decree and declare that as I delight myself in You, You will grant me the desires of my heart, as written in Psalm 37:4. I trust You to lead me to the man You have prepared for me.

2. Lord, I declare that I will recognize a godly man by his fruits, for Your Word says, 'By their fruit you will recognize them' (Matthew 7:16). I ask for discernment to see beyond appearances.

3. I decree that I will not settle for less than Your best, for Your Word says, 'For I know the plans I have for you, declares the Lord, plans to prosper you and not to harm you' (Jeremiah 29:11). I trust in Your perfect plan.

4. Father, I declare that my future husband will be a man of faith, for Your Word says, 'But without faith it is impossible to please Him' (Hebrews 11:6). His life will reflect trust in You.

5. Lord, I decree that my future husband will be a man who walks in wisdom, for Your Word says, 'The fear of the Lord is the beginning of wisdom' (Proverbs 9:10). His decisions will be guided by reverence for You.

6. I declare that I will be hidden in You, Lord, so that my future husband must seek You to find me, for Your Word says, 'Your life is now hidden with Christ in God' (Colossians 3:3). I remain secure in Your presence.

7. Father, I decree that I will not be deceived by counterfeits, for Your Word says, 'Do not judge according to appearance, but judge with righteous judgment' (John 7:24). I ask for clarity and discernment.

8. Lord, I declare that my future husband will honor me as his wife, for Your Word says, 'Husbands, love your wives and do not be harsh with them' (Colossians 3:19). He will treat me with respect and kindness.

9. I decree that my future husband will walk in humility, for Your Word says, 'Humble yourselves before the Lord, and He will lift you up' (James 4:10). He will lead with a servant's heart.

10. Father, I declare that my future husband will be a man of prayer, for Your Word says, 'The prayer of a righteous person is powerful and effective' (James 5:16). His life will be rooted in intercession.

11. Lord, I decree that my future husband will have a heart for Your Word, for Your Word says, 'Your Word is a lamp to my feet and a light to my path' (Psalm 119:105). He will walk in alignment with Your truth.

12. I declare that I will not be anxious about finding a spouse, for Your Word says, 'Do not be anxious about anything, but in every situation, by prayer and petition, with thanksgiving, present your requests to God' (Philippians 4:6). I rest in Your timing.

13. Father, I decree that my future husband will be a man of integrity, for Your Word says, 'The righteous man walks in his

integrity; his children are blessed after him' (Proverbs 20:7). He will lead with honor.

14. Lord, I declare that my future husband will have a vision for his life, for Your Word says, 'Where there is no vision, the people perish' (Proverbs 29:18). He will pursue Your purpose.

15. I decree that I will walk in purity as I wait, for Your Word says, 'Blessed are the pure in heart, for they will see God' (Matthew 5:8). I consecrate myself to You.

16. Father, I declare that my future husband will love You with all his heart, soul, and mind, for Your Word says, 'Love the Lord your God with all your heart and with all your soul and with all your mind' (Matthew 22:37). His life will reflect his devotion to You.

17. Lord, I decree that my future husband will be patient and kind, for Your Word says, 'Love is patient, love is kind' (1 Corinthians 13:4). His character will mirror Your love.

18. I declare that my future husband will walk in the fruit of the Spirit, for Your Word says, 'The fruit of the Spirit is love, joy, peace, forbearance, kindness, goodness, faithfulness, gentleness, and self-control' (Galatians 5:22-23). He will exhibit these qualities.

19. Father, I decree that my future husband will be a man of courage, for Your Word says, 'Be strong and courageous. Do not be afraid; do not be discouraged, for the Lord your God will be with you wherever you go' (Joshua 1:9). He will lead boldly.

20. Lord, I declare that I will trust Your timing and plan for my future husband, for Your Word says, 'He has made everything beautiful in its time' (Ecclesiastes 3:11). I surrender my desires to You.

**Closing Prayer:**

Father, I thank You for the man You are preparing for me. Align my heart with Your will and prepare me to be the spouse You desire. Remove every distraction and counterfeit, and let my trust remain in You. May my future husband be a man who honors You in all he does, and may our union glorify Your name. In Jesus' name, Amen.

# SECTION 4

# PREPARING FOR MARRIAGE

# CHAPTER 27

# Declarations to find a Godly Woman

**Scripture Focus:**
*"Who can find a virtuous wife? For her worth is far above rubies."*
*Proverbs 31:10 (NKJV)*

**Introduction:**

Finding a godly woman is not about superficial qualities but about aligning with God's divine blueprint for a virtuous partner. Proverbs 31:10 describes the priceless value of a wife who walks in wisdom, faith, and purpose. This chapter equips men with declarations to discern, attract, and prepare for a godly woman who complements their purpose and honors God.

## 20 Declarations to Find a Godly Woman

1. Father, in the name of Jesus, I decree and declare that I will find a virtuous wife, for Your Word says, 'Who can find a virtuous wife? For her worth is far above rubies' (Proverbs 31:10). I trust You to lead me to the right woman.

2. Lord, I declare that I will recognize a godly woman by her fruits, for Your Word says, 'By their fruit you will know them' (Matthew 7:16). Give me discernment to see her heart.

3. I decree that I will not be led by appearances alone, for Your Word says, 'Charm is deceitful and beauty is passing, but a woman who fears the Lord, she shall be praised' (Proverbs 31:30). I value her character above all.

4. Father, I declare that my future wife will love You above all else, for Your Word says, 'Love the Lord your God with all your heart and with all your soul and with all your mind' (Matthew 22:37). Her devotion will be to You first.

5. Lord, I decree that my future wife will walk in wisdom, for Your Word says, 'She opens her mouth with wisdom, and on her tongue is the law of kindness' (Proverbs 31:26). She will speak life and truth.

6. I declare that I will seek Your guidance in choosing a wife, for Your Word says, 'Trust in the Lord with all your heart and lean not on your own understanding' (Proverbs 3:5). I will rely on Your wisdom.

7. Father, I decree that my future wife will be a woman of prayer, for Your Word says, 'Pray without ceasing' (1 Thessalonians 5:17). Her life will be rooted in intercession.

8. Lord, I declare that my future wife will walk in humility, for Your Word says, 'Do nothing out of selfish ambition or vain conceit. Rather, in humility value others above yourselves' (Philippians 2:3). She will reflect Christ's character.

9. I decree that my future wife will be a woman of strength and dignity, for Your Word says, 'She is clothed with strength and dignity; she can laugh at the days to come' (Proverbs 31:25). She will be resilient and joyful.

10. Father, I declare that my future wife will be a builder of her home, for Your Word says, 'The wise woman builds her house, but the foolish pulls it down with her hands' (Proverbs 14:1). She will steward her responsibilities with wisdom.

11. Lord, I decree that my future wife will support and encourage my purpose, for Your Word says, 'Two are better than one, because they have a good return for their labor' (Ecclesiastes 4:9). Together, we will fulfill Your will.

12. I declare that my future wife will be patient and kind, for Your Word says, 'Love is patient, love is kind' (1 Corinthians 13:4). Her love will reflect Your nature.

13. Father, I decree that my future wife will walk in purity and holiness, for Your Word says, 'Blessed are the pure in heart, for they will see God' (Matthew 5:8). She will be consecrated to You.

14. Lord, I declare that my future wife will be a peacemaker, for Your Word says, 'Blessed are the peacemakers, for they shall be called sons of God' (Matthew 5:9). She will cultivate harmony in our home.

15. I decree that my future wife will have a heart of service, for Your Word says, 'Serve one another humbly in love' (Galatians 5:13). She will serve joyfully and selflessly.

16. Father, I declare that my future wife will raise our children in Your ways, for Your Word says, 'Train up a child in the way he should go, and when he is old he will not depart from it' (Proverbs 22:6). She will nurture them in faith.

17. Lord, I decree that I will not be deceived by counterfeits, for Your Word says, 'Do not judge according to appearance, but judge with righteous judgment' (John 7:24). I will discern with Your wisdom.

18. I declare that my future wife will walk in joy, for Your Word says, 'The joy of the Lord is your strength' (Nehemiah 8:10). Her life will radiate gladness.

19. Father, I decree that my future wife will partner with me in building a home that honors You, for Your Word says, 'Unless the Lord builds the house, the builders labor in vain' (Psalm 127:1). Our home will glorify You.

20. Lord, I declare that I will wait patiently for the woman You have chosen for me, for Your Word says, 'He has made everything

beautiful in its time' (Ecclesiastes 3:11). I trust in Your perfect timing.

**Closing Prayer:**

Father, I thank You for preparing a godly woman who will be my partner in life and faith. Align my heart with Yours as I wait for Your appointed time. Bless her wherever she is and prepare her for the covenant we will share. Let our union glorify You and advance Your Kingdom. In Jesus' name, Amen.

# CHAPTER 28

# Declarations to Break Cycles of Distrust

***Scripture Focus:***
*"Trust in the Lord with all your heart*
*and lean not on your own understanding."*
*Proverbs 3:5 (NKJV)*

**Introduction:**
Distrust, whether caused by past hurts, betrayals, or fears, can become a cycle that hinders relationships and the ability to move forward. Proverbs 3:5 calls believers to trust fully in the Lord, relinquishing self-reliance and allowing Him to heal and restore. Breaking cycles of distrust requires surrender to God's truth and speaking His promises into your heart and mind.

These declarations will empower you to release old wounds, embrace healing, and walk in trust — first with God, then with others.

## 20 Declarations to Break Cycles of Distrust

1. Father, in the name of Jesus, I decree and declare that I will trust in You with all my heart, as Your Word says in Proverbs 3:5. I let go of my own understanding and rely on Your unfailing guidance.

2. Lord, I declare that every root of distrust in my heart is uprooted, for Your Word says, 'Every plant that my heavenly Father has not planted will be pulled up by the roots' (Matthew 15:13). I submit my heart to Your healing.

3. I decree that I am free from the fear of betrayal, for Your Word says, 'God has not given us a spirit of fear, but of power, and of love, and of a sound mind' (2 Timothy 1:7). I walk in boldness and trust.

4. Father, I declare that past betrayals no longer have power over me, for Your Word says, 'Forget the former things; do not dwell on the past' (Isaiah 43:18). I embrace the new thing You are doing in my life.

5. Lord, I decree that I will trust in Your plans for my relationships, for Your Word says, 'For I know the plans I have for you, declares the Lord, plans to prosper you and not to harm you' (Jeremiah 29:11). I surrender to Your purpose.

6. I declare that I will not judge others by my past experiences, for Your Word says, 'Do not judge by appearances, but judge with right judgment' (John 7:24). I choose discernment over suspicion.

7. Father, I decree that I will walk in the freedom of forgiveness, for Your Word says, 'Bear with each other and forgive one another... Forgive as the Lord forgave you' (Colossians 3:13). I release every offense.

8. Lord, I declare that my mind is renewed, for Your Word says, 'Be transformed by the renewing of your mind, that you may prove what is that good and acceptable and perfect will of God' (Romans 12:2). I think with clarity and truth.

9. I decree that I will no longer carry the weight of suspicion, for Your Word says, 'Cast all your anxiety on Him because He cares for you' (1 Peter 5:7). I release all burdens to You.

10. Father, I declare that I am rooted in Your love, for Your Word says, 'Love bears all things, believes all things, hopes all things, endures all things' (1 Corinthians 13:7). I choose to believe the best in others.

11. Lord, I decree that I will trust again, for Your Word says, 'The Lord is my strength and my shield; my heart trusts in Him, and He helps me' (Psalm 28:7). My heart will not harden.

12. I declare that my heart is guarded by Your peace, for Your Word says, 'And the peace of God, which transcends all understanding, will guard your hearts and your minds in Christ Jesus' (Philippians 4:7). I am free from turmoil.

13. Father, I decree that I will discern the truth in every relationship, for Your Word says, 'The Spirit of truth... will guide you into all truth' (John 16:13). I rely on Your Spirit for guidance.

14. Lord, I declare that I will not sabotage healthy relationships, for Your Word says, 'Let us not become weary in doing good, for at the proper time we will reap a harvest if we do not give up' (Galatians 6:9). I will persevere in love.

15. I decree that I will walk in the freedom of Christ, for Your Word says, 'If the Son sets you free, you will be free indeed' (John 8:36). I am no longer bound by distrust.

16. Father, I declare that I will trust others without fear, for Your Word says, 'Love does no harm to a neighbor. Therefore love is the fulfillment of the law' (Romans 13:10). I will choose love over fear.

17. Lord, I decree that I will release every hurt to You, for Your Word says, 'Come to me, all you who are weary and burdened, and I will give you rest' (Matthew 11:28). I find rest in You.

18. I declare that my relationships will be restored, for Your Word says, 'He restores my soul; He leads me in paths of righteousness for His name's sake' (Psalm 23:3). I walk in restoration.

19. Father, I decree that I will trust in Your justice, for Your Word says, 'It is mine to avenge; I will repay, says the Lord' (Romans 12:19). I release every desire for vengeance.

20. Lord, I declare that I will walk in truth and love, for Your Word says, 'Let us not love with words or speech but with actions and in truth' (1 John 3:18). My relationships will reflect Your glory.

**Closing Prayer:**

Father, I thank You for breaking the cycle of distrust in my heart and life. Heal every wound, restore my faith in others, and renew my mind with Your truth. Let my relationships be rooted in love, trust, and grace. May my life be a reflection of Your restoration power. In Jesus' name, Amen.

# CHAPTER 29

# Declarations to Break Emotional Baggage

**Scripture Focus:**
*"Cast all your anxiety on Him because He cares for you."*
*1 Peter 5:7 (NIV)*

**Introduction:**
Emotional baggage can weigh heavily on the heart, hindering relationships and blocking the ability to fully embrace God's plans. The Word of God calls us to cast our burdens on Him, trusting in His care and releasing what no longer serves His purpose in our lives. This chapter focuses on breaking free from past hurts, disappointments, and unresolved pain to step into a future unburdened and full of promise.

## 20 Declarations to Break Emotional Baggage

1. Father, in the name of Jesus, I decree and declare that every burden I carry is released to You, for Your Word says, 'Cast all your anxiety on Him because He cares for you' (1 Peter 5:7). I surrender all my pain to You.

2. Lord, I declare that my heart is healed, for Your Word says, 'He heals the brokenhearted and binds up their wounds' (Psalm 147:3). My past no longer defines me.

3. I decree that I will not carry the weight of past relationships, for Your Word says, 'Forget the former things; do not dwell on the past' (Isaiah 43:18). I step into the new thing You are doing.

4. Father, I declare that every root of bitterness is uprooted from my heart, for Your Word says, 'See to it that no one falls short of the grace of God and that no bitter root grows up to cause trouble' (Hebrews 12:15). I release all unforgiveness.

5. Lord, I decree that I am free from guilt and shame, for Your Word says, 'Those who look to Him are radiant; their faces are never covered with shame' (Psalm 34:5). I walk in the light of Your grace.

6. I declare that I will no longer replay past hurts, for Your Word says, 'As far as the east is from the west, so far has He removed our transgressions from us' (Psalm 103:12). I let go of every painful memory.

7. Father, I decree that I am free from fear of vulnerability, for Your Word says, 'There is no fear in love. But perfect love drives out fear' (1 John 4:18). I trust in Your perfect love.

8. Lord, I declare that I will no longer hold on to rejection, for Your Word says, 'Even if my father and mother abandon me, the Lord will hold me close' (Psalm 27:10, NLT). I am fully accepted in You.

9. I decree that I will walk in peace, for Your Word says, 'The Lord gives strength to His people; the Lord blesses His people with peace' (Psalm 29:11). My heart is at rest in You.

10. Father, I declare that I will forgive myself for past mistakes, for Your Word says, 'There is now no condemnation for those who are in Christ Jesus' (Romans 8:1). I am free from self-blame.

11. Lord, I decree that my emotions are submitted to You, for Your Word says, 'And the peace of God, which transcends all understanding, will guard your hearts and your minds in Christ Jesus' (Philippians 4:7). My heart and mind are protected.

12. I declare that every soul tie from my past is broken, for Your Word says, 'Do not be yoked together with unbelievers' (2 Corinthians 6:14). I am free to move forward in purity.

13. Father, I decree that I will walk in joy, for Your Word says, 'The joy of the Lord is your strength' (Nehemiah 8:10). My joy is restored in You.

14. Lord, I declare that I will embrace my future with hope, for

Your Word says, 'For I know the plans I have for you, declares the Lord, plans to prosper you and not to harm you, plans to give you hope and a future' (Jeremiah 29:11). My future is secure in You.

15. I decree that I will not carry the pain of childhood wounds, for Your Word says, 'When I was a child, I spoke like a child, I thought like a child, I reasoned like a child. When I became a man, I gave up childish ways' (1 Corinthians 13:11). I release every hurt from my past.

16. Father, I declare that I am a new creation, for Your Word says, 'If anyone is in Christ, the new creation has come: The old has gone, the new is here!' (2 Corinthians 5:17). I walk in newness of life.

17. Lord, I decree that my identity is rooted in You, for Your Word says, 'See what great love the Father has lavished on us, that we should be called children of God!' (1 John 3:1). I am not defined by my past.

18. I declare that every burden is lifted, for Your Word says, 'Come to me, all you who are weary and burdened, and I will give you rest' (Matthew 11:28). I rest in Your presence.

19. Father, I decree that I will no longer feel unworthy, for Your Word says, 'You are precious and honored in my sight, and I love you' (Isaiah 43:4). I am loved and valued by You.

20. Lord, I declare that I will step boldly into freedom, for Your Word says, 'It is for freedom that Christ has set us free. Stand

firm, then, and do not let yourselves be burdened again by a yoke of slavery' (Galatians 5:1). I claim my freedom in You.

**Closing Prayer:**
Father, I thank You for breaking the chains of emotional baggage in my life. Heal every wound, restore my joy, and renew my mind. Let me walk boldly in freedom, fully embracing the plans You have for me. In Jesus' name, Amen.

# CHAPTER 30

# Declarations to Reverse Curses Spoken Over You

**Scripture Focus:**
*"Like a fluttering sparrow or a darting swallow, an undeserved curse does not come to rest."*
*Proverbs 26:2 (NIV)*

**Introduction:**
Words spoken against us can carry spiritual weight, especially when rooted in malice or bitterness. However, as children of God, we are not subject to curses but empowered to break them through the authority of Christ. Proverbs 26:2 assures us that undeserved curses cannot take root. By declaring God's promises, we can reverse every spoken curse and replace it with His blessings.

These declarations will dismantle every word curse, revoke its effects, and establish God's divine will in your life.

## 20 Declarations to Reverse Curses Spoken Over You

1. Father, in the name of Jesus, I decree and declare that every curse spoken over my life is reversed, for Your Word says, 'Like a fluttering sparrow or a darting swallow, an undeserved curse does not come to rest' (Proverbs 26:2). No weapon formed against me shall prosper.

2. Lord, I declare that every word of condemnation is broken, for Your Word says, 'There is therefore now no condemnation for those who are in Christ Jesus' (Romans 8:1). I walk in freedom and grace.

3. I decree that every generational curse is destroyed, for Your Word says, 'Christ redeemed us from the curse of the law by becoming a curse for us' (Galatians 3:13). I am set free by the blood of Jesus.

4. Father, I declare that I am blessed and not cursed, for Your Word says, 'The Lord will bless you and keep you; the Lord make His face shine upon you and be gracious to you' (Numbers 6:24-25). Your blessing rests on me.

5. Lord, I decree that every negative word spoken against my destiny is nullified, for Your Word says, 'You will refute every tongue that accuses you. This is the heritage of the servants of the Lord' (Isaiah 54:17). I stand in my heritage of protection.

6. I declare that my life is shielded by Your truth, for Your Word says, 'You are my hiding place; You will protect me from trouble and surround me with songs of deliverance' (Psalm 32:7). No curse can touch me.

7. Father, I decree that every curse of failure is replaced with success, for Your Word says, 'Whatever he does prospers' (Psalm 1:3). I am fruitful in all my endeavors.

8. Lord, I declare that every word of rejection is reversed, for Your Word says, 'Even if my father and mother abandon me, the Lord will hold me close' (Psalm 27:10). I am accepted in Your love.

9. I decree that every curse of sickness is broken, for Your Word says, 'By His stripes, we are healed' (Isaiah 53:5). I walk in divine health and wholeness.

10. Father, I declare that I am protected from the schemes of the enemy, for Your Word says, 'No weapon formed against you shall prosper' (Isaiah 54:17). Every attack is nullified.

11. Lord, I decree that every curse of poverty is reversed, for Your Word says, 'The Lord will open the heavens, the storehouse of His bounty, to send rain on your land in season and to bless all the work of your hands' (Deuteronomy 28:12). I walk in abundance.

12. I declare that my identity is secure in You, for Your Word says, 'But you are a chosen generation, a royal priesthood, a holy nation, His own special people' (1 Peter 2:9). No word can diminish my worth.

13. Father, I decree that every spoken word of fear is replaced with faith, for Your Word says, 'God has not given us a spirit of fear, but of power and of love and of a sound mind' (2 Timothy 1:7). I walk in courage.

14. Lord, I declare that every curse of confusion is broken, for Your Word says, 'For God is not the author of confusion but of peace' (1 Corinthians 14:33). My mind is clear and focused.

15. I decree that my life is a reflection of Your blessings, for Your Word says, 'Blessed shall you be when you come in, and blessed shall you be when you go out' (Deuteronomy 28:6). I am blessed in every season.

16. Father, I declare that every curse of barrenness is broken, for Your Word says, 'He makes the barren woman abide in the house as a joyful mother of children' (Psalm 113:9). I am fruitful in every area of life.

17. Lord, I decree that every curse of stagnation is reversed, for Your Word says, 'Forget the former things; do not dwell on the past. See, I am doing a new thing!' (Isaiah 43:18-19). I move forward in Your purpose.

18. I declare that my words will align with Your truth, for Your Word says, 'The tongue has the power of life and death, and those who love it will eat its fruit' (Proverbs 18:21). I speak life over myself.

19. Father, I decree that my future is secure, for Your Word says, 'For I know the plans I have for you, declares the Lord, plans to prosper you and not to harm you' (Jeremiah 29:11). I will fulfill my destiny.

20. Lord, I declare that I am an overcomer, for Your Word says,

'They triumphed over him by the blood of the Lamb and by the word of their testimony' (Revelation 12:11). I walk in victory.

**Closing Prayer:**
Father, I thank You for reversing every curse spoken over my life. I stand on Your Word, which is my shield and defense. Let Your blessings replace every curse, and let my life reflect Your glory. In Jesus' name, Amen.

# CHAPTER 31

# Declarations for Grace to Be Single

**Scripture Focus:**
*"My grace is sufficient for you, for my power is made perfect in weakness."*
*2 Corinthians 12:9 (NIV)*

**Introduction:**

Singleness is not a limitation but a season filled with purpose, growth, and preparation. God's grace is sufficient to sustain and empower you, allowing you to walk confidently in this season. 2 Corinthians 12:9 reminds us that His power is magnified in our areas of need, and in singleness, His strength provides peace, fulfillment, and focus.

These declarations equip you to embrace singleness as a time of divine favor and preparation, allowing God to refine you for His purposes.

## 20 Declarations for Grace to Be Single

1. Father, in the name of Jesus, I decree and declare that Your grace is sufficient for me in this season of singleness, for Your Word says, 'My grace is sufficient for you, for my power is made perfect in weakness' (2 Corinthians 12:9). I rely on Your strength.

2. Lord, I declare that I am complete in You, for Your Word says, 'And you are complete in Him, who is the head of all principality and power' (Colossians 2:10). I lack nothing in this season.

3. I decree that my singleness is a season of purpose, for Your Word says, 'To everything there is a season, a time for every purpose under heaven' (Ecclesiastes 3:1). I align myself with Your divine timing.

4. Father, I declare that I will delight in You, for Your Word says, 'Delight yourself also in the Lord, and He shall give you the desires of your heart' (Psalm 37:4). My joy is found in Your presence.

5. Lord, I decree that I will not feel alone, for Your Word says, 'I will never leave you nor forsake you' (Hebrews 13:5). I am surrounded by Your love.

6. I declare that I will walk in holiness and purity, for Your Word says, 'But just as He who called you is holy, so be holy in all you do' (1 Peter 1:15). I consecrate myself to You.

7. Father, I decree that I will use this season to grow in wisdom, for Your Word says, 'The fear of the Lord is the beginning of

wisdom' (Proverbs 9:10). I pursue a deeper relationship with You.

8. Lord, I declare that I will be content in this season, for Your Word says, 'I have learned to be content whatever the circumstances' (Philippians 4:11). My heart is at peace.

9. I decree that I will guard my heart, for Your Word says, 'Above all else, guard your heart, for everything you do flows from it' (Proverbs 4:23). My focus remains on You.

10. Father, I declare that I will not waste this season, for Your Word says, 'So teach us to number our days, that we may gain a heart of wisdom' (Psalm 90:12). I will maximize this time for Your glory.

11. Lord, I decree that I will walk in joy, for Your Word says, 'The joy of the Lord is your strength' (Nehemiah 8:10). My singleness is a season of joy.

12. I declare that I will trust Your timing, for Your Word says, 'He has made everything beautiful in its time' (Ecclesiastes 3:11). I wait patiently on You.

13. Father, I decree that I am fruitful in this season, for Your Word says, 'He shall be like a tree planted by the rivers of water, that brings forth its fruit in its season' (Psalm 1:3). I thrive in this time.

14. Lord, I declare that I will focus on serving You, for Your Word says, 'But seek first the kingdom of God and His righteousness, and all these things shall be added to you' (Matthew 6:33). My priority is Your Kingdom.

wisdom' (Proverbs 9:10). I pursue a deeper relationship with You.

8. Lord, I declare that I will be content in this season, for Your Word says, 'I have learned to be content whatever the circumstances' (Philippians 4:11). My heart is at peace.

9. I decree that I will guard my heart, for Your Word says, 'Above all else, guard your heart, for everything you do flows from it' (Proverbs 4:23). My focus remains on You.

10. Father, I declare that I will not waste this season, for Your Word says, 'So teach us to number our days, that we may gain a heart of wisdom' (Psalm 90:12). I will maximize this time for Your glory.

11. Lord, I decree that I will walk in joy, for Your Word says, 'The joy of the Lord is your strength' (Nehemiah 8:10). My singleness is a season of joy.

12. I declare that I will trust Your timing, for Your Word says, 'He has made everything beautiful in its time' (Ecclesiastes 3:11). I wait patiently on You.

13. Father, I decree that I am fruitful in this season, for Your Word says, 'He shall be like a tree planted by the rivers of water, that brings forth its fruit in its season' (Psalm 1:3). I thrive in this time.

14. Lord, I declare that I will focus on serving You, for Your Word says, 'But seek first the kingdom of God and His righteousness, and all these things shall be added to you' (Matthew 6:33). My priority is Your Kingdom.

15. I decree that I will walk in peace, for Your Word says, 'And the peace of God, which transcends all understanding, will guard your hearts and your minds in Christ Jesus' (Philippians 4:7). My heart is secure in You.

16. Father, I declare that I will grow in spiritual maturity, for Your Word says, 'But grow in the grace and knowledge of our Lord and Savior Jesus Christ' (2 Peter 3:18). This season will strengthen my faith.

17. Lord, I decree that I will not be swayed by societal pressures, for Your Word says, 'Do not conform to the pattern of this world, but be transformed by the renewing of your mind' (Romans 12:2). My identity is rooted in You.

18. I declare that I will prepare myself for the future, for Your Word says, 'She watches over the affairs of her household and does not eat the bread of idleness' (Proverbs 31:27). I am proactive and diligent.

19. Father, I decree that I will use this season to glorify You, for Your Word says, 'Whatever you do, do it all for the glory of God' (1 Corinthians 10:31). My singleness is an offering to You.

20. Lord, I declare that I will embrace Your purpose for this season, for Your Word says, 'For we are God's handiwork, created in Christ Jesus to do good works, which God prepared in advance for us to do' (Ephesians 2:10). I fulfill Your plan for my life.

**Closing Prayer:**

Father, I thank You for the grace to walk confidently in this season of singleness. Help me to grow, serve, and glorify You in all that I do. I trust in Your perfect timing and plan for my life. Let Your joy and peace fill my heart, and may this season prepare me for all You have ordained. In Jesus' name, Amen.

# CHAPTER 32

# Declarations and Repentance for Sexual Impurity

**Scripture Focus:**
*"Flee sexual immorality. Every sin that a man does is outside the body, but he who commits sexual immorality sins against his own body."*
*1 Corinthians 6:18 (NKJV)*

**Introduction:**
Sexual purity is not just an act but a heart posture before God. The Bible calls us to flee from immorality, as it defiles the body, which is the temple of the Holy Spirit. Repentance is the first step toward healing and restoration, and through the blood of Jesus, every stain of impurity can be cleansed.

These declarations and prayers for repentance are designed to guide you through surrendering your heart, breaking free from cycles of impurity, and walking in holiness.

## 20 Declarations and Prayers of Repentance for Sexual Impurity

1. Father, I repent for every act of sexual impurity, for Your Word says, 'If we confess our sins, He is faithful and just to forgive us our sins and to cleanse us from all unrighteousness' (1 John 1:9). I ask for Your forgiveness and cleansing.

2. Lord, I decree that my body is a temple of the Holy Spirit, for Your Word says, 'Do you not know that your body is the temple of the Holy Spirit who is in you?' (1 Corinthians 6:19). I consecrate my body to You.

3. I declare that I will flee from every temptation, for Your Word says, 'No temptation has overtaken you except what is common to mankind. And God is faithful; He will not let you be tempted beyond what you can bear' (1 Corinthians 10:13). I walk in Your strength.

4. Father, I decree that every chain of addiction to sexual sin is broken, for Your Word says, 'So if the Son sets you free, you will be free indeed' (John 8:36). I walk in total freedom.

5. Lord, I repent for entertaining impure thoughts, for Your Word says, 'Finally, brothers and sisters, whatever is true, whatever is noble, whatever is right... think about such things' (Philippians 4:8). I surrender my mind to You.

6. I declare that I will walk in holiness, for Your Word says, 'But just as He who called you is holy, so be holy in all you do' (1 Peter 1:15). I am set apart for Your glory.

7. Father, I decree that my past does not define me, for Your Word says, 'Therefore, if anyone is in Christ, the new creation has come: The old has gone, the new is
here!' (2 Corinthians 5:17). I am made new in You.

8. Lord, I declare that I will guard my eyes, for Your Word says, 'I have made a covenant with my eyes; why then should I look upon a young woman?' (Job 31:1). I choose purity in what I see.

9. I decree that every unholy soul tie is broken, for Your Word says, 'What therefore God has joined together, let no man separate' (Matthew 19:6). I sever every ungodly connection.

10. Father, I repent for every misuse of my body, for Your Word says, 'Offer your bodies as a living sacrifice, holy and pleasing to God—this is your true and proper worship' (Romans 12:1). I surrender my body to You.

11. Lord, I declare that I am clothed in righteousness, for Your Word says, 'I delight greatly in the Lord; my soul rejoices in my God. For He has clothed me with garments of salvation' (Isaiah 61:10). I am covered by Your grace.

12. I decree that I will meditate on Your Word daily, for Your Word says, 'How can a young man cleanse his way? By taking heed according to Your word' (Psalm 119:9). I fill my heart with Your truth.

13. Father, I declare that I will not be conformed to this world, for Your Word says, 'Do not conform to the pattern of this world, but be transformed by the renewing of your mind' (Romans 12:2). My mind is renewed by You.

14. Lord, I decree that I am no longer a slave to sin, for Your Word says, 'For sin shall no longer be your master, because you are not under the law, but under grace' (Romans 6:14). I walk in Your grace.

15. I declare that I will set boundaries to protect my purity, for Your Word says, 'Do not give the devil a foothold' (Ephesians 4:27). I guard my life from compromise.

16. Father, I repent for lustful desires, for Your Word says, 'Put to death, therefore, whatever belongs to your earthly nature: sexual immorality, impurity, lust, evil desires' (Colossians 3:5). I crucify my flesh in Your power.

17. Lord, I decree that I will walk in accountability, for Your Word says, 'Confess your sins to one another, and pray for one another, that you may be healed' (James 5:16). I seek godly counsel.

18. I declare that my heart is pure, for Your Word says, 'Blessed are the pure in heart, for they shall see God' (Matthew 5:8). I desire to see You in my life.

19. Father, I decree that I will resist the devil, for Your Word says, 'Submit yourselves, then, to God. Resist the devil, and he will flee from you' (James 4:7). I stand firm in Your authority.

20. Lord, I declare that I will glorify You in my body, for Your Word says, 'Therefore glorify God in your body and in your spirit, which are God's' (1 Corinthians 6:20). My life reflects Your holiness.

**Closing Prayer:**

Father, I repent of every act, thought, and word that has not honored You. Cleanse me by Your blood and renew my spirit. Break every chain of impurity, and empower me to walk in holiness and righteousness. Let my life glorify You in every way. In Jesus' name, Amen.

# CHAPTER 33

# Declarations Against Pornography and Lust for Him

*Scripture Focus:*
*"I have made a covenant with my eyes;*
*why then should I look upon a young woman?"*
*Job 31:1 (NKJV)*

**Introduction:**

The battle against pornography and lust is one of the most pervasive struggles for men today. However, God's Word provides both the authority and the tools to overcome these temptations. Job 31:1 reminds us of the importance of guarding our eyes and hearts, committing them to holiness.

These declarations equip men to renounce lust, break free from the chains of pornography, and live in purity, empowered by the truth of God's Word.

## 20 Declarations Against Pornography and Lust

1. Father, in the name of Jesus, I decree and declare that I have made a covenant with my eyes, as Job declared in Job 31:1. I will not set my gaze on anything impure.

2. Lord, I declare that my body is a temple of the Holy Spirit, for Your Word says, 'Do you not know that your body is the temple of the Holy Spirit?' (1 Corinthians 6:19). I dedicate my body and mind to You.

3. I decree that I will walk in purity, for Your Word says, 'Blessed are the pure in heart, for they shall see God' (Matthew 5:8). My heart and thoughts are consecrated to You.

4. Father, I declare that I will not conform to the patterns of this world, for Your Word says, 'Do not conform to the pattern of this world, but be transformed by the renewing of your mind' (Romans 12:2). My mind is renewed by Your truth.

5. Lord, I decree that every stronghold of pornography is broken in my life, for Your Word says, 'The weapons of our warfare are not carnal but mighty in God for pulling down strongholds' (2 Corinthians 10:4). I destroy every lie of the enemy.

6. I declare that I will flee from temptation, for Your Word says, 'Flee sexual immorality. Every sin that a man does is outside the body' (1 Corinthians 6:18). I turn away from every snare.

7. Father, I decree that my thoughts are pure, for Your Word says, 'Finally, brothers and sisters, whatever is true, whatever is noble,

whatever is right, whatever is pure... think about such things' (Philippians 4:8). I fix my mind on what honors You.

8. Lord, I declare that every unholy desire is crucified, for Your Word says, 'Those who belong to Christ Jesus have crucified the flesh with its passions and desires' (Galatians 5:24). I walk in the Spirit and not the flesh.

9. I decree that I will resist the devil, for Your Word says, 'Submit yourselves, then, to God. Resist the devil, and he will flee from you' (James 4:7). I stand firm against every attack.

10. Father, I declare that I will guard my eyes and ears, for Your Word says, 'The eye is the lamp of the body. If your eyes are healthy, your whole body will be full of light' (Matthew 6:22). I choose to focus on Your light.

11. Lord, I decree that I am not a slave to sin, for Your Word says, 'For sin shall no longer be your master, because you are not under the law, but under grace' (Romans 6:14). I walk in the freedom of Your grace.

12. I declare that my identity is rooted in You, for Your Word says, 'If anyone is in Christ, he is a new creation. The old has passed away; behold, the new has come' (2 Corinthians 5:17). I live as a new creation in Christ.

13. Father, I decree that I will meditate on Your Word day and night, for Your Word says, 'Your word I have hidden in my heart, that I might not sin against You' (Psalm 119:11). Your Word is my shield against temptation.

14. Lord, I declare that every chain of addiction is broken, for Your Word says, 'So if the Son sets you free, you will be free indeed' (John 8:36). I am free from the bondage of lust.

15. I decree that I will surround myself with godly accountability, for Your Word says, 'Confess your sins to each other and pray for each other so that you may be healed' (James 5:16). I invite trusted brothers to walk with me in purity.

16. Father, I declare that my marriage (or future marriage) will be protected, for Your Word says, 'Marriage should be honored by all, and the marriage bed kept
pure' (Hebrews 13:4). I will honor my spouse with integrity.

17. Lord, I decree that my spirit is stronger than my flesh, for Your Word says, 'Watch and pray so that you will not fall into temptation. The spirit is willing, but the flesh is weak' (Matthew 26:41). I strengthen my spirit through prayer.

18. I declare that I will walk in humility and repentance, for Your Word says, 'If we confess our sins, He is faithful and just to forgive us our sins and to cleanse us from all unrighteousness' (1 John 1:9). I confess and receive Your forgiveness.

19. Father, I decree that I will walk in the fruit of self-control, for Your Word says, 'But the fruit of the Spirit is love, joy, peace… self-control' (Galatians 5:22-23). My life reflects the fruit of Your Spirit.

20. Lord, I declare that my life will glorify You, for Your Word says, 'Whatever you do, do it all for the glory of God' (1

Corinthians 10:31). My body, mind, and spirit honor You in all things.

**Closing Prayer:**

Father, I thank You for breaking the power of pornography and lust over my life. I commit my eyes, thoughts, and desires to You, choosing purity and holiness. Strengthen me daily to walk in Your light and truth. Let my life glorify You in every way. In Jesus' name, Amen.

# CHAPTER 34

# Declarations Against Pornography and Lust for Her

**Scripture Focus:**
*"You have heard that it was said, 'You shall not commit adultery.' But I tell you that anyone who looks at a woman lustfully has already committed adultery with her in his heart."*
*Matthew 5:27-28 (NIV)*

**Introduction:**

Lust is not limited by gender; it affects women as much as men, though often overlooked. Jesus emphasized the sanctity of our thoughts and intentions, calling us to purity in both heart and mind. Breaking free from pornography and lust requires surrender, repentance, and the power of God's Word to renew the mind and spirit.

These declarations are designed to empower women to overcome lust, reject pornography, and walk in holiness and freedom.

## 20 Declarations Against Pornography and Lust for Her

1. Father, in the name of Jesus, I decree and declare that I will guard my heart and mind, for Your Word says, 'Above all else, guard your heart, for everything you do flows from it' (Proverbs 4:23). My thoughts are consecrated to You.

2. Lord, I declare that I will not look upon anything that defiles, for Your Word says, 'I will set no wicked thing before my eyes' (Psalm 101:3). I fix my eyes on what is pure.

3. I decree that every stronghold of lust is broken in my life, for Your Word says, 'The weapons of our warfare are not carnal but mighty in God for pulling down strongholds' (2 Corinthians 10:4). I walk in freedom.

4. Father, I declare that I am no longer a slave to sin, for Your Word says, 'For sin shall no longer be your master, because you are not under the law, but under grace' (Romans 6:14). I am free from the bondage of lust.

5. Lord, I decree that my thoughts will align with Your truth, for Your Word says, 'Finally, brothers and sisters, whatever is true, whatever is noble, whatever is right... think about such things' (Philippians 4:8). My mind is renewed by Your Word.

6. I declare that I will walk in purity, for Your Word says, 'Blessed are the pure in heart, for they shall see God' (Matthew 5:8). My heart is set on You.

7. Father, I decree that every chain of addiction is broken, for

Your Word says, 'So if the Son sets you free, you will be free indeed' (John 8:36). I walk in complete liberty.

8. Lord, I declare that I will flee from temptation, for Your Word says, 'Flee from sexual immorality. Every other sin a person commits is outside the body' (1 Corinthians 6:18). I turn away from every trap of the enemy.

9. I decree that I will walk in accountability, for Your Word says, 'Confess your sins to one another and pray for one another, that you may be healed' (James 5:16). I seek godly support and counsel.

10. Father, I declare that my identity is rooted in You, for Your Word says, 'You are a chosen people, a royal priesthood, a holy nation, God's special possession' (1 Peter 2:9). I am secure in Your love.

11. Lord, I decree that I will not conform to the standards of this world, for Your Word says, 'Do not conform to the pattern of this world, but be transformed by the renewing of your mind' (Romans 12:2). My life reflects Your kingdom.

12. I declare that every unholy desire is crucified, for Your Word says, 'Those who belong to Christ Jesus have crucified the flesh with its passions and desires' (Galatians 5:24). I walk in the Spirit.

13. Father, I decree that I will meditate on Your Word, for Your Word says, 'Your word I have hidden in my heart, that I might not sin against You' (Psalm 119:11). Your truth is my defense.

14. Lord, I declare that my body is a temple of the Holy Spirit, for Your Word says, 'Do you not know that your body is a temple of the Holy Spirit?' (1 Corinthians 6:19). I honor You with my body.

15. I decree that I will walk in self-control, for Your Word says, 'For God gave us a spirit not of fear but of power and love and self-control' (2 Timothy 1:7). I am disciplined in my thoughts and actions.

16. Father, I declare that I will not entertain unclean media or influences, for Your Word says, 'Do not give the devil a foothold' (Ephesians 4:27). I guard my life against compromise.

17. Lord, I decree that I will reflect Your love and purity, for Your Word says, 'Be imitators of God, as beloved children' (Ephesians 5:1). My life is a mirror of Your holiness.

18. I declare that my heart and mind will be filled with Your peace, for Your Word says, 'The peace of God, which transcends all understanding, will guard your hearts and your minds in Christ Jesus' (Philippians 4:7). I rest in Your peace.

19. Father, I decree that I will resist every attack of the enemy, for Your Word says, 'Submit yourselves, then, to God. Resist the devil, and he will flee from you' (James 4:7). I stand firm in Your power.

20. Lord, I declare that I will glorify You in all that I do, for Your Word says, 'Whatever you do, do it all for the glory of God' (1 Corinthians 10:31). My life honors You in every way.

**Closing Prayer:**

Father, I surrender my thoughts, desires, and actions to You. Break every chain of lust and pornography in my life and renew my heart with Your holiness. Help me to walk in freedom, accountability, and peace, reflecting Your purity in all I do. In Jesus' name, Amen.

# CHAPTER 35

# Spiritual Warfare Declarations for Singles

***Scripture Focus:***
*"For we do not wrestle against flesh and blood, but against principalities, against powers, against the rulers of the darkness of this age, against spiritual hosts of wickedness in the heavenly places."*
*Ephesians 6:12 (NKJV)*

**Introduction:**
Singleness is often a season of great spiritual battles, as the enemy seeks to sow discouragement, distraction, and discontentment. However, God has equipped believers with the authority to wage war in the spirit and overcome every attack of the enemy. Ephesians 6:12 reminds us that the true fight is not physical but spiritual, and through Christ, we have victory.

These declarations are tools of spiritual warfare, empowering singles to overcome the enemy's schemes and stand firm in faith and purpose.

## 20 Spiritual Warfare Declarations for Singles

1. Father, in the name of Jesus, I decree and declare that I am strong in You and in the power of Your might, for Your Word says, 'Put on the full armor of God so that you can take your stand against the devil's schemes' (Ephesians 6:11). I stand equipped for battle.

2. Lord, I declare that every scheme of the enemy against my singleness is exposed and defeated, for Your Word says, 'No weapon formed against you shall prosper' (Isaiah 54:17). I walk in victory.

3. I decree that I take every thought captive to the obedience of Christ, for Your Word says, 'We demolish arguments and every pretension that sets itself up against the knowledge of God' (2 Corinthians 10:5). My mind is fortified in You.

4. Father, I declare that I am protected by the shield of faith, for Your Word says, 'Take up the shield of faith, with which you can extinguish all the flaming arrows of the evil one' (Ephesians 6:16). My faith is unshakable.

5. Lord, I decree that I stand firm against every lie of the enemy, for Your Word says, 'You will know the truth, and the truth will set you free' (John 8:32). I walk in the freedom of Your truth.

6. I declare that I am clothed in the righteousness of Christ, for Your Word says, 'Stand firm then, with the belt of truth buckled around your waist and the breastplate of righteousness in place' (Ephesians 6:14). I am secure in Your covering.

7. Father, I decree that every generational curse is broken, for Your Word says, 'Christ redeemed us from the curse of the law by becoming a curse for us' (Galatians 3:13). I am free through Your sacrifice.

8. Lord, I declare that my prayers are powerful and effective, for Your Word says, 'The prayer of a righteous person is powerful and effective' (James 5:16). I declare breakthroughs in the spirit.

9. I decree that I am victorious over every temptation, for Your Word says, 'God is faithful; He will not let you be tempted beyond what you can bear' (1 Corinthians 10:13). I triumph in Your strength.

10. Father, I declare that every spirit of delay is defeated, for Your Word says, 'The vision is yet for an appointed time... it will surely come' (Habakkuk 2:3). I walk in Your perfect timing.

11. Lord, I decree that every spirit of discouragement is broken, for Your Word says, 'Do not be afraid or discouraged, for the Lord your God is with you wherever you go' (Joshua 1:9). I am filled with courage and hope.

12. I declare that every chain of stagnation is destroyed, for Your Word says, 'Break every yoke' (Isaiah 58:6). I move forward into Your purpose.

13. Father, I decree that I am surrounded by Your angelic protection, for Your Word says, 'For He will command His angels concerning you to guard you in all your ways' (Psalm 91:11). I am shielded on every side.

14. Lord, I declare that I walk in the light, for Your Word says, 'The light shines in the darkness, and the darkness has not overcome it' (John 1:5). No darkness can prevail against me.

15. I decree that my destiny is secure, for Your Word says, 'For I know the plans I have for you... plans to prosper you and not to harm you' (Jeremiah 29:11). I fulfill every divine assignment.

16. Father, I declare that every voice of condemnation is silenced, for Your Word says, 'There is now no condemnation for those who are in Christ Jesus' (Romans 8:1). I walk in confidence and grace.

17. Lord, I decree that my steps are ordered by You, for Your Word says, 'The steps of a good man are ordered by the Lord' (Psalm 37:23). I follow Your divine direction.

18. I declare that I am a conqueror, for Your Word says, 'In all these things we are more than conquerors through Him who loved us' (Romans 8:37). I walk in Your victory.

19. Father, I decree that I stand firm in the Word of God, for Your Word says, 'Heaven and earth will pass away, but My words will never pass away' (Matthew 24:35). I am unshakable in Your truth.

20. Lord, I declare that I walk in spiritual authority, for Your Word says, 'I have given you authority to trample on snakes and scorpions and to overcome all the power of the enemy' (Luke 10:19). I exercise my authority in Christ.

**Closing Prayer:**

Father, I thank You for equipping me with the tools of spiritual warfare. I stand firm in Your Word, resisting every attack of the enemy. Let my life be a testimony of Your power, protection, and victory. In Jesus' name, Amen.

# SECTION 5

# PROTECTING MARRIAGE AND FAMILY

# CHAPTER 36

# Declarations for Wisdom to Build a Home

*Scripture Focus:*
*"By wisdom a house is built, and through understanding it is established."*
*Proverbs 24:3 (NIV)*

**Introduction:**
Building a home requires more than physical structures—it is a spiritual and emotional endeavor rooted in wisdom and understanding. Proverbs 24:3 reminds us that wisdom is the foundation of a thriving household. These declarations will help you seek divine wisdom, understanding, and grace to establish a home that reflects God's principles and peace.

## 20 Declarations for Wisdom to Build a Home

1. Father, in the name of Jesus, I decree and declare that my home is built on Your wisdom, for Your Word says, 'By wisdom a house is built, and through understanding it is established' (Proverbs 24:3). I rely on Your guidance.

2. Lord, I declare that my home will reflect Your peace, for Your Word says, 'Blessed are the peacemakers, for they will be called children of God' (Matthew 5:9). I will cultivate harmony in every relationship.

3. I decree that my household will be rooted in love, for Your Word says, 'Above all, love each other deeply, because love covers over a multitude of sins' (1 Peter 4:8). Love will be the foundation of my home.

4. Father, I declare that I will lead my home with understanding, for Your Word says, 'Get wisdom, get understanding; do not forget my words or turn away from them' (Proverbs 4:5). I will seek Your counsel daily.

5. Lord, I decree that my family will walk in unity, for Your Word says, 'How good and pleasant it is when God's people live together in unity!' (Psalm 133:1). My home will be a place of togetherness.

6. I declare that I will speak life into my household, for Your Word says, 'The tongue has the power of life and death' (Proverbs 18:21). My words will edify and encourage.

7. Father, I decree that my home will be a place of prayer, for Your Word says, 'My house will be called a house of prayer for all nations' (Isaiah 56:7). I will prioritize communion with You.

8. Lord, I declare that my household will walk in obedience to Your Word, for Your Word says, 'As for me and my house, we will serve the Lord' (Joshua 24:15). Our lives will honor You.

9. I decree that every member of my household will fulfill their purpose, for Your Word says, 'For we are God's handiwork, created in Christ Jesus to do good works' (Ephesians 2:10). Our home will nurture destiny.

10. Father, I declare that my home will reflect Your light, for Your Word says, 'You are the light of the world. A town built on a hill cannot be hidden' (Matthew 5:14). Our lives will testify of Your goodness.

11. Lord, I decree that my home will be a place of joy, for Your Word says, 'The joy of the Lord is your strength' (Nehemiah 8:10). Joy will strengthen every member of my household.

12. I declare that my home will be free from strife, for Your Word says, 'Better a dry crust with peace and quiet than a house full of feasting, with strife' (Proverbs 17:1). Peace will reign within our walls.

13. Father, I decree that I will steward my household with diligence, for Your Word says, 'The wise woman builds her house, but with her own hands the foolish one tears hers down' (Proverbs 14:1). I will be intentional in my actions.

14. Lord, I declare that every decision in my home will be guided by You, for Your Word says, 'Trust in the Lord with all your heart and lean not on your own understanding' (Proverbs 3:5). I surrender my plans to You.

15. I decree that my home will be a place of generosity, for Your Word says, 'A generous person will prosper; whoever refreshes others will be refreshed' (Proverbs 11:25). We will give freely and abundantly.

16. Father, I declare that my household will model forgiveness, for Your Word says, 'Bear with each other and forgive one another if any of you has a grievance against someone' (Colossians 3:13). Forgiveness will be our standard.

17. Lord, I decree that my home will be protected by Your angels, for Your Word says, 'For He will command His angels concerning you to guard you in all your ways' (Psalm 91:11). Your divine protection surrounds us.

18. I declare that my home will be a place of faith, for Your Word says, 'For we walk by faith, not by sight' (2 Corinthians 5:7). We will trust in Your promises.

19. Father, I decree that my household will leave a legacy of righteousness, for Your Word says, 'The righteous man walks in his integrity; his children are blessed after him' (Proverbs 20:7). Generations will be blessed by our example.

20. Lord, I declare that my home will be established on Your Word, for Your Word says, 'Everyone who hears these words of

mine and puts them into practice is like a wise man who built his house on the rock' (Matthew 7:24). Our foundation is unshakable.

**Closing Prayer:**

Father, I thank You for the wisdom, understanding, and grace to build a home that honors You. Let every word, action, and decision in my household reflect Your love and truth. Establish my home on the firm foundation of Your Word, and may it be a place of peace, joy, and purpose. In Jesus' name, Amen.

# CHAPTER 37

# Declarations for Family Disputes Against Your Spouse

**Scripture Focus:**
*"A wise woman builds her home, but a foolish woman tears it down with her own hands."*
*Proverbs 14:1 (NLT)*

**Introduction:**
Family disputes can often strain relationships, especially when external family members create conflict. God's Word encourages wisdom, unity, and peace in managing disputes, ensuring that the sanctity of marriage remains protected. Proverbs 14:1 highlights the role of wisdom in building and sustaining a home. These declarations equip you to navigate family challenges with grace, ensuring that your relationship with your spouse remains fortified against external pressures.

## 20 Declarations for Family Disputes Against Your Spouse

1. Father, in the name of Jesus, I decree and declare that my marriage is shielded from external strife, for Your Word says, 'What God has joined together, let no one separate' (Matthew 19:6). Our bond is unbreakable.

2. Lord, I declare that my home will be a place of peace, for Your Word says, 'Blessed are the peacemakers, for they will be called children of God' (Matthew 5:9). I will pursue peace in every dispute.

3. I decree that I will walk in wisdom, for Your Word says, 'If any of you lacks wisdom, you should ask God, who gives generously to all without finding fault, and it will be given to you' (James 1:5). I seek Your wisdom in managing family conflicts.

4. Father, I declare that my words will build up and not tear down, for Your Word says, 'Do not let any unwholesome talk come out of your mouths, but only what is helpful for building others up' (Ephesians 4:29). I speak life into my marriage.

5. Lord, I decree that I will honor my spouse, for Your Word says, 'Honor one another above yourselves' (Romans 12:10). I will always protect and uphold their dignity.

6. I declare that no weapon formed against my marriage shall prosper, for Your Word says, 'No weapon forged against you will prevail, and you will refute every tongue that accuses you' (Isaiah 54:17). Every plan of division is nullified.

7. Father, I decree that I will act with understanding and compassion, for Your Word says, 'Be kind and compassionate to one another, forgiving each other, just as in Christ God forgave you' (Ephesians 4:32). I choose love over conflict.

8. Lord, I declare that my family will not sow discord in my marriage, for Your Word says, 'There are six things the Lord hates... a person who stirs up conflict in the community' (Proverbs 6:16-19). Peace will reign in my home.

9. I decree that my marriage will be a testimony of unity, for Your Word says, 'Make every effort to keep the unity of the Spirit through the bond of peace' (Ephesians 4:3). We are one in You.

10. Father, I declare that I will handle disagreements with love, for Your Word says, 'Hatred stirs up conflict, but love covers over all wrongs' (Proverbs 10:12). I will love unconditionally.

11. Lord, I decree that every spirit of misunderstanding is silenced, for Your Word says, 'Where there is strife, there is pride, but wisdom is found in those who take advice' (Proverbs 13:10). I will walk humbly in wisdom.

12. I declare that my home is protected from gossip and slander, for Your Word says, 'A perverse person stirs up conflict, and a gossip separates close friends' (Proverbs 16:28). No evil word will take root in my heart or home.

13. Father, I decree that I will honor my in-laws while prioritizing my spouse, for Your Word says, 'For this reason, a man will leave his father and mother and be united to his wife' (Genesis 2:24).

Our marriage is the priority.

14. Lord, I declare that I will extend grace in conflict, for Your Word says, 'Let your conversation be always full of grace, seasoned with salt' (Colossians 4:6). My responses will be gentle and wise.

15. I decree that every root of bitterness is uprooted, for Your Word says, 'See to it that no one falls short of the grace of God and that no bitter root grows up to cause trouble and defile many' (Hebrews 12:15). My heart is free from bitterness.

16. Father, I declare that I will listen more and speak less, for Your Word says, 'Everyone should be quick to listen, slow to speak and slow to become angry' (James 1:19). I will listen with understanding.

17. Lord, I decree that my marriage is covered by Your protection, for Your Word says, 'The name of the Lord is a fortified tower; the righteous run to it and are safe' (Proverbs 18:10). You are our refuge.

18. I declare that I will not repay evil with evil, for Your Word says, 'Do not repay anyone evil for evil. Be careful to do what is right in the eyes of everyone' (Romans 12:17). I will respond with grace.

19. Father, I decree that I will prioritize prayer in every conflict, for Your Word says, 'Pray in the Spirit on all occasions with all kinds of prayers and requests' (Ephesians 6:18). I will seek You first.

20. Lord, I declare that my marriage will glorify You, for Your Word says, 'So whether you eat or drink or whatever you do, do it all for the glory of God' (1 Corinthians 10:31). Our union reflects Your glory.

**Closing Prayer:**

Father, I thank You for the gift of marriage and for the wisdom to navigate family conflicts with grace. Protect my marriage from strife, gossip, and division. Let peace, understanding, and unity prevail in every situation. May my actions and words always reflect Your love. In Jesus' name, Amen.

# CHAPTER 38

## Declarations to Break Ungodly Soul Ties with a Controlling Father

***Scripture Focus:***
*"You shall know the truth, and the truth shall make you free."*
*John 8:32 (NKJV)*

**Introduction:**
Ungodly soul ties can hinder freedom and spiritual growth, especially when tied to controlling relationships. While honoring parents is biblical, control and manipulation are not of God. John 8:32 reminds us that truth brings freedom. Breaking these ties requires recognizing the unhealthy dynamics and submitting them to God for healing and restoration.

These declarations empower you to break free from ungodly control and walk in the liberty Christ has given you.

# 20 Declarations to Break Ungodly Soul Ties with a Controlling Father

1. Father, in the name of Jesus, I decree and declare that every ungodly soul tie with a controlling father is broken, for Your Word says, 'You shall know the truth, and the truth shall make you free' (John 8:32). I walk in freedom.

2. Lord, I declare that I am no longer bound by control, for Your Word says, 'It is for freedom that Christ has set us free. Stand firm, then, and do not let yourselves be burdened again by a yoke of slavery' (Galatians 5:1). I will not return to bondage.

3. I decree that I honor my father as commanded, but I reject manipulation and control, for Your Word says, 'Honor your father and your mother, so that you may live long in the land the Lord your God is giving you' (Exodus 20:12). I separate honor from control.

4. Father, I declare that I am free from fear of disapproval, for Your Word says, 'For God has not given us a spirit of fear, but of power and of love and of a sound mind' (2 Timothy 1:7). I live boldly in Your truth.

5. Lord, I decree that every controlling word spoken over my life is nullified, for Your Word says, 'No weapon formed against you shall prosper, and you will refute every tongue that accuses you' (Isaiah 54:17). I refute every negative word.

6. I declare that my identity is rooted in You, for Your Word says, 'See what great love the Father has lavished on us, that we should

be called children of God!' (1 John 3:1). My worth is defined by You alone.

7. Father, I decree that I will walk in obedience to Your will, for Your Word says, 'We must obey God rather than human beings' (Acts 5:29). I prioritize Your commands above human expectations.

8. Lord, I declare that every emotional chain tied to manipulation is broken, for Your Word says, 'The Lord is close to the brokenhearted and saves those who are crushed in spirit' (Psalm 34:18). You restore my soul.

9. I decree that I am no longer controlled by guilt, for Your Word says, 'There is therefore now no condemnation for those who are in Christ Jesus' (Romans 8:1). I walk free of condemnation.

10. Father, I declare that I will walk in healthy boundaries, for Your Word says, 'Above all else, guard your heart, for everything you do flows from it' (Proverbs 4:23). I protect my heart from manipulation.

11. Lord, I decree that my mind is renewed, for Your Word says, 'Do not conform to the pattern of this world, but be transformed by the renewing of your mind' (Romans 12:2). I think according to Your truth.

12. I declare that I am free to pursue my God-given purpose, for Your Word says, 'For I know the plans I have for you, declares the Lord, plans to prosper you and not to harm you' (Jeremiah 29:11). I follow Your plans for my life.

13. Father, I decree that every generational pattern of control is broken, for Your Word says, 'Christ redeemed us from the curse of the law by becoming a curse for us' (Galatians 3:13). I am free from inherited cycles.

14. Lord, I declare that I will forgive my father, for Your Word says, 'Forgive as the Lord forgave you' (Colossians 3:13). I release every offense into Your hands.

15. I decree that my emotions are healed, for Your Word says, 'He heals the brokenhearted and binds up their wounds' (Psalm 147:3). My heart is whole in You.

16. Father, I declare that I will honor You above all, for Your Word says, 'You shall have no other gods before Me' (Exodus 20:3). My allegiance is to You alone.

17. Lord, I decree that I will speak truth in love, for Your Word says, 'Instead, speaking the truth in love, we will grow to become in every respect the mature body of Him who is the head, that is, Christ' (Ephesians 4:15). My words will be guided by love and wisdom.

18. I declare that I am free from false responsibility, for Your Word says, 'Come to me, all you who are weary and burdened, and I will give you rest' (Matthew 11:28). I rest in Your freedom.

19. Father, I decree that I will walk in the fruit of the Spirit, for Your Word says, 'The fruit of the Spirit is love, joy, peace, forbearance, kindness, goodness, faithfulness, gentleness, and self-control' (Galatians 5:22-23). My actions reflect Your Spirit.

20. Lord, I declare that I am free to walk in Your truth, for Your Word says, 'Then you will know the truth, and the truth will set you free' (John 8:32). I live in the liberty of Your truth.

**Closing Prayer:**

Father, I thank You for breaking every ungodly soul tie with a controlling father. I honor my earthly father while rejecting manipulation and control. Heal my heart, renew my mind, and help me walk in the freedom and purpose You have designed for me. In Jesus' name, Amen.

# CHAPTER 39

# Declarations to Break Ungodly Soul Ties with a Controlling Mother

**Scripture Focus:**
*"For the Lord is the Spirit, and wherever the Spirit of the Lord is, there is freedom."*
*2 Corinthians 3:17 (NLT)*

**Introduction:**
A controlling mother can create emotional and spiritual entanglements that hinder personal growth and independence. While the Bible commands us to honor our parents, it also teaches that true freedom is found in Christ. Breaking ungodly soul ties with a controlling mother allows you to honor her without being bound by manipulation or unhealthy dependency.

These declarations guide you in severing these ties, seeking healing, and walking in the freedom that Christ provides.

**20 Declarations to Break Ungodly Soul Ties with a Controlling Mother**

1. Father, in the name of Jesus, I decree and declare that every ungodly soul tie with a controlling mother is broken, for Your Word says, 'Where the Spirit of the Lord is, there is freedom' (2 Corinthians 3:17). I walk in Your freedom.

2. Lord, I declare that I honor my mother without yielding to manipulation, for Your Word says, 'Honor your father and your mother, so that you may live long in the land the Lord your God is giving you' (Exodus 20:12). I choose to honor with wisdom.

3. I decree that I will not be bound by guilt or obligation, for Your Word says, 'It is for freedom that Christ has set us free. Stand firm, then, and do not let yourselves be burdened again by a yoke of slavery' (Galatians 5:1). I am free from false responsibilities.

4. Father, I declare that every word curse spoken over my life is broken, for Your Word says, 'The tongue has the power of life and death' (Proverbs 18:21). I reject every negative word.

5. Lord, I decree that my identity is secure in You, for Your Word says, 'But you are a chosen people, a royal priesthood, a holy nation, God's special possession' (1 Peter 2:9). My worth is defined by You alone.

6. I declare that I am no longer controlled by fear, for Your Word says, 'For God has not given us a spirit of fear, but of power and of love and of a sound mind' (2 Timothy 1:7). I walk in Your power and love.

7. Father, I decree that my emotions are healed, for Your Word says, 'He heals the brokenhearted and binds up their wounds' (Psalm 147:3). My heart is whole in You.

8. Lord, I declare that I will walk in healthy boundaries, for Your Word says, 'Above all else, guard your heart, for everything you do flows from it' (Proverbs 4:23). I will protect my heart from manipulation.

9. I decree that I am free from emotional entanglements, for Your Word says, 'So if the Son sets you free, you will be free indeed' (John 8:36). I live in complete liberty.

10. Father, I declare that I will forgive my mother for any hurt caused, for Your Word says, 'Bear with each other and forgive one another if any of you has a grievance against someone. Forgive as the Lord forgave you' (Colossians 3:13). I release her into Your hands.

11. Lord, I decree that every spirit of control is silenced, for Your Word says, 'Submit yourselves, then, to God. Resist the devil, and he will flee from you' (James 4:7). I resist every influence that is not of You.

12. I declare that I will obey You above all, for Your Word says, 'We must obey God rather than human beings' (Acts 5:29). Your voice is my ultimate authority.

13. Father, I decree that every generational pattern of control is broken, for Your Word says, 'Christ redeemed us from the curse of the law by becoming a curse for us' (Galatians 3:13). I am free

from inherited cycles.

14. Lord, I declare that I will walk in truth, for Your Word says, 'Then you will know the truth, and the truth will set you free' (John 8:32). Your truth governs my life.

15. I decree that I will walk in peace, for Your Word says, 'The peace of God, which transcends all understanding, will guard your hearts and your minds in Christ Jesus' (Philippians 4:7). Peace reigns in my heart and mind.

16. Father, I declare that I will speak truth in love, for Your Word says, 'Speaking the truth in love, we will grow to become in every respect the mature body of Him who is the head, that is, Christ' (Ephesians 4:15). My words will be guided by love and wisdom.

17. Lord, I decree that I will walk in Your purpose for my life, for Your Word says, 'For I know the plans I have for you, declares the Lord, plans to prosper you and not to harm you' (Jeremiah 29:11). I fulfill Your divine assignment.

18. I declare that I am protected from manipulation, for Your Word says, 'The Lord is my rock, my fortress and my deliverer; my God is my rock, in whom I take refuge' (Psalm 18:2). You are my shield and defense.

19. Father, I decree that I will extend grace to my mother while walking in truth, for Your Word says, 'Let your conversation be always full of grace, seasoned with salt' (Colossians 4:6). I balance grace and conviction.

20. Lord, I declare that my relationship with my mother is restored to Your design, for Your Word says, 'He restores my soul; He leads me in paths of righteousness for His name's sake' (Psalm 23:3). Healing and restoration flow in my family.

**Closing Prayer:**

Father, I thank You for breaking every ungodly soul tie with a controlling mother. I release every hurt and manipulation into Your hands. Heal my heart, renew my spirit, and help me to honor her in a way that reflects Your love and truth. In Jesus' name, Amen.

# CHAPTER 40

# Declarations Over a Child Born Through Sexual Sin

**Scripture Focus:**
*"Before I formed you in the womb I knew you,
before you were born I set you apart."
Jeremiah 1:5 (NIV)*

**Introduction:**
A child's identity and purpose are ordained by God, regardless of the circumstances of their conception. Jeremiah 1:5 assures us that every life is known, valued, and set apart by the Creator. Speaking blessings and affirmations over a child born through sexual sin is a powerful way to cancel any shame or stigma and affirm God's plan for their life.

These declarations will speak life, purpose, and destiny into the child, establishing their identity in Christ and securing their future in God's hands.

# 20 Declarations Over a Child Born Through Sexual Sin

1. Father, in the name of Jesus, I decree and declare that this child is fearfully and wonderfully made, for Your Word says, 'I praise You because I am fearfully and wonderfully made; Your works are wonderful' (Psalm 139:14). They are a masterpiece of Your creation.

2. Lord, I declare that this child is known and loved by You, for Your Word says, 'Before I formed you in the womb I knew you, before you were born I set you apart' (Jeremiah 1:5). Their life is purposed by You.

3. I decree that every spirit of shame or rejection is broken, for Your Word says, 'There is therefore now no condemnation for those who are in Christ
Jesus' (Romans 8:1). This child is free from condemnation.

4. Father, I declare that this child is a blessing, for Your Word says, 'Children are a heritage from the Lord, offspring a reward from Him' (Psalm 127:3). They are a reward from You.

5. Lord, I decree that this child's future is secure, for Your Word says, 'For I know the plans I have for you... plans to prosper you and not to harm you, plans to give you hope and a future' (Jeremiah 29:11). Their destiny is bright.

6. I declare that this child is covered by Your love, for Your Word says, 'The Lord your God is with you, the Mighty Warrior who saves. He will take great delight in you; in His love He will no longer rebuke you, but will rejoice over you with singing' (Zephaniah 3:17). They are deeply cherished.

7. Father, I decree that no curse or stigma will attach itself to this child, for Your Word says, 'Christ redeemed us from the curse of the law by becoming a curse for us' (Galatians 3:13). They walk in freedom.

8. Lord, I declare that this child will walk in wisdom, for Your Word says, 'If any of you lacks wisdom, you should ask God, who gives generously to all without finding fault' (James 1:5). They will make wise decisions.

9. I decree that this child will be a vessel of honor, for Your Word says, 'Those who cleanse themselves... will be instruments for special purposes, made holy, useful to the Master' (2 Timothy 2:21). They are set apart for You.

10. Father, I declare that this child will be surrounded by godly influences, for Your Word says, 'Walk with the wise and become wise, for a companion of fools suffers harm' (Proverbs 13:20). They will be mentored by the righteous.

11. Lord, I decree that this child will fulfill every God-given purpose, for Your Word says, 'The Lord will fulfill His purpose for me; Your steadfast love, O Lord, endures forever' (Psalm 138:8). Their destiny will not be delayed or denied.

12. I declare that this child is protected from harm, for Your Word says, 'The Lord will watch over your coming and going both now and forevermore' (Psalm 121:8). They are covered by Your hand.

13. Father, I decree that this child will be a light in the world, for Your Word says, 'You are the light of the world. A town built on a

hill cannot be hidden' (Matthew 5:14). They will shine with Your glory.

14. Lord, I declare that this child will know their identity in You, for Your Word says, 'But you are a chosen people, a royal priesthood, a holy nation, God's special possession' (1 Peter 2:9). They are Yours.

15. I decree that every negative word spoken against this child is canceled, for Your Word says, 'You will refute every tongue that accuses you. This is the heritage of the servants of the Lord' (Isaiah 54:17). No word curse will prevail.

16. Father, I declare that this child will grow in favor with God and man, for Your Word says, 'And Jesus grew in wisdom and stature, and in favor with God and man' (Luke 2:52). Their life will reflect Your grace.

17. Lord, I decree that this child's steps are ordered by You, for Your Word says, 'The steps of a good man are ordered by the Lord' (Psalm 37:23). They will walk in divine alignment.

18. I declare that this child will be a voice for Your Kingdom, for Your Word says, 'Go into all the world and preach the gospel to all creation' (Mark 16:15). They will boldly proclaim Your truth.

19. Father, I decree that this child will walk in love, for Your Word says, 'Let all that you do be done in love' (1 Corinthians 16:14). Their life will be marked by compassion and kindness.

20. Lord, I declare that this child will glorify You in all they do, for

Your Word says, 'So whether you eat or drink or whatever you do, do it all for the glory of God' (1 Corinthians 10:31). Their life will honor You.

**Closing Prayer:**
Father, I thank You for the life of this child, who is a precious gift from You. I cancel every stigma, curse, or lie spoken against them. Let their life shine with Your purpose, love, and glory. Surround them with Your protection, favor, and wisdom as they grow into the person You've created them to be. In Jesus' name, Amen.

# CHAPTER 41

# Declarations for feelings of Shame, fear, and Guilt

*Scripture Focus:*
*"Those who look to Him are radiant;
their faces are never covered with shame."
Psalm 34:5 (NIV)*

**Introduction:**
Shame, fear, and guilt are tools the enemy uses to keep believers bound and separated from God's love. However, through Christ, we have been set free from condemnation and called to live in the light of His truth. Psalm 34:5 reminds us that those who turn to God are radiant and unashamed.

These declarations are a powerful way to reject shame, fear, and guilt, and embrace the freedom, peace, and joy that Christ provides.

## 20 Declarations for Feelings of Shame, Fear, and Guilt

1. Father, in the name of Jesus, I decree and declare that I look to You and am radiant, for Your Word says, 'Those who look to Him are radiant; their faces are never covered with shame' (Psalm 34:5). I walk in Your light.

2. Lord, I declare that I am free from condemnation, for Your Word says, 'There is therefore now no condemnation for those who are in Christ Jesus' (Romans 8:1). I reject guilt and shame.

3. I decree that I am forgiven, for Your Word says, 'If we confess our sins, He is faithful and just to forgive us our sins and to purify us from all unrighteousness' (1 John 1:9). I am cleansed by Your blood.

4. Father, I declare that fear has no hold on me, for Your Word says, 'For God has not given us a spirit of fear, but of power and of love and of a sound mind' (2 Timothy 1:7). I walk in courage and power.

5. Lord, I decree that I am covered by Your love, for Your Word says, 'Perfect love drives out fear, because fear has to do with punishment' (1 John 4:18). I rest in Your perfect love.

6. I declare that I am accepted by You, for Your Word says, 'Accept one another, then, just as Christ accepted you, in order to bring praise to God' (Romans 15:7). I am embraced by Your grace.

7. Father, I decree that my past does not define me, for Your Word says, 'Therefore, if anyone is in Christ, the new creation has

come: The old has gone, the new is here!' (2 Corinthians 5:17). I am made new in You.

8. Lord, I declare that I will not be anxious, for Your Word says, 'Do not be anxious about anything, but in every situation, by prayer and petition, with thanksgiving, present your requests to God' (Philippians 4:6). I cast all my cares on You.

9. I decree that shame is removed from my life, for Your Word says, 'Instead of your shame, you will receive a double portion, and instead of disgrace, you will rejoice in your inheritance' (Isaiah 61:7). I receive Your honor and blessing.

10. Father, I declare that I am clothed in Your righteousness, for Your Word says, 'I delight greatly in the Lord; my soul rejoices in my God. For He has clothed me with garments of salvation and arrayed me in a robe of His righteousness' (Isaiah 61:10). I am covered by Your glory.

11. Lord, I decree that every lie of the enemy is silenced, for Your Word says, 'The thief comes only to steal and kill and destroy; I have come that they may have life, and have it to the full' (John 10:10). I choose Your abundant life.

12. I declare that I will not dwell on my mistakes, for Your Word says, 'Forget the former things; do not dwell on the past' (Isaiah 43:18). I focus on the new thing You are doing.

13. Father, I decree that I walk in peace, for Your Word says, 'The peace of God, which transcends all understanding, will guard your hearts and your minds in Christ Jesus' (Philippians 4:7). My mind is guarded by Your peace.

14. Lord, I declare that I am bold in Your presence, for Your Word says, 'In Him and through faith in Him we may approach God with freedom and confidence' (Ephesians 3:12). I come before You without fear.

15. I decree that I am healed from every emotional wound, for Your Word says, 'He heals the brokenhearted and binds up their wounds' (Psalm 147:3). My heart is restored.

16. Father, I declare that I am victorious over every accusation, for Your Word says, 'Who will bring any charge against those whom God has chosen? It is God who justifies' (Romans 8:33). I stand justified in You.

17. Lord, I decree that I am strong in You, for Your Word says, 'The Lord is my light and my salvation—whom shall I fear? The Lord is the stronghold of my life—of whom shall I be afraid?' (Psalm 27:1). You are my strength.

18. I declare that I am filled with joy, for Your Word says, 'The joy of the Lord is your strength' (Nehemiah 8:10). Joy fills every area of my life.

19. Father, I decree that I will walk in truth, for Your Word says, 'Then you will know the truth, and the truth will set you free' (John 8:32). I embrace the freedom of Your truth.

20. Lord, I declare that I am free to live fully in You, for Your Word says, 'If the Son sets you free, you will be free indeed' (John 8:36). I walk in complete liberty through Christ.

**Closing Prayer:**

Father, I thank You for lifting the weight of shame, fear, and guilt from my life. I rest in the assurance of Your love and forgiveness. Let Your peace guard my heart and mind as I walk boldly in Your truth. In Jesus' name, Amen.

# CHAPTER 42

# Declarations to War Against Satan's Wicked Thoughts

***Scripture Focus:***
*"We demolish arguments and every pretension that sets itself up against the knowledge of God, and we take captive every thought to make it obedient to Christ."*
*2 Corinthians 10:5 (NIV)*

**Introduction:**

The mind is often the battleground where the enemy sows lies, doubt, and wicked thoughts. However, God has equipped believers with divine authority to take every thought captive and bring it under the obedience of Christ. Spiritual warfare begins with recognizing the enemy's tactics and using the Word of God to counter every lie.

These declarations empower you to demolish strongholds in your mind and replace Satan's wicked thoughts with God's truth and peace.

## 20 Declarations to War Against Satan's Wicked Thoughts

1. Father, in the name of Jesus, I decree and declare that every wicked thought is demolished, for Your Word says, 'We demolish arguments and every pretension that sets itself up against the knowledge of God' (2 Corinthians 10:5). My mind is guarded by Your truth.

2. Lord, I declare that I will take every thought captive, for Your Word says, 'Take captive every thought to make it obedient to Christ' (2 Corinthians 10:5). My thoughts align with Your Word.

3. I decree that I will reject every lie of the enemy, for Your Word says, 'The thief comes only to steal and kill and destroy; I have come that they may have life, and have it to the full' (John 10:10). I embrace Your abundant life.

4. Father, I declare that my mind is renewed daily, for Your Word says, 'Do not conform to the pattern of this world, but be transformed by the renewing of your mind' (Romans 12:2). I walk in renewed understanding.

5. Lord, I decree that I will meditate on what is pure and true, for Your Word says, 'Whatever is true, whatever is noble, whatever is right, whatever is pure... think about such things' (Philippians 4:8). My thoughts reflect Your purity.

6. I declare that I have the mind of Christ, for Your Word says, 'We have the mind of Christ' (1 Corinthians 2:16). I think with divine wisdom.

7. Father, I decree that I am protected from the fiery darts of the enemy, for Your Word says, 'Take up the shield of faith, with which you can extinguish all the flaming arrows of the evil one' (Ephesians 6:16). My faith is my defense.

8. Lord, I declare that every argument of fear is silenced, for Your Word says, 'For God has not given us a spirit of fear, but of power and of love and of a sound mind' (2 Timothy 1:7). I walk in boldness and clarity.

9. I decree that I will not entertain thoughts of condemnation, for Your Word says, 'There is therefore now no condemnation for those who are in Christ
Jesus' (Romans 8:1). I live free from guilt.

10. Father, I declare that I am strengthened by Your Word, for Your Word says, 'The Lord is my light and my salvation—whom shall I fear? The Lord is the stronghold of my life—of whom shall I be afraid?' (Psalm 27:1). I am fearless in You.

11. Lord, I decree that I will resist every thought of inadequacy, for Your Word says, 'I can do all things through Christ who strengthens me' (Philippians 4:13). I am equipped for every task.

12. I declare that every thought of defeat is replaced with victory, for Your Word says, 'But thanks be to God! He gives us the victory through our Lord Jesus Christ' (1 Corinthians 15:57). I walk in triumph.

13. Father, I decree that my thoughts are filled with peace, for

Your Word says, 'You will keep in perfect peace those whose minds are steadfast, because they trust in You' (Isaiah 26:3). Peace guards my mind.

14. Lord, I declare that every stronghold of confusion is destroyed, for Your Word says, 'For God is not a God of confusion but of peace' (1 Corinthians 14:33). My mind is clear and focused.

15. I decree that I will trust in Your promises, for Your Word says, 'Trust in the Lord with all your heart and lean not on your own understanding' (Proverbs 3:5). My mind rests in You.

16. Father, I declare that I am filled with Your light, for Your Word says, 'The light shines in the darkness, and the darkness has not overcome it' (John 1:5). Darkness cannot prevail in my life.

17. Lord, I decree that I will rebuke every voice of the accuser, for Your Word says, 'The accuser of our brothers and sisters... has been hurled down' (Revelation 12:10). I silence the voice of accusation.

18. I declare that I will not be anxious, for Your Word says, 'Do not be anxious about anything, but in every situation, by prayer and petition, with thanksgiving, present your requests to God' (Philippians 4:6). Anxiety has no place in my life.

19. Father, I decree that I will stand firm in Your Word, for Your Word says, 'Heaven and earth will pass away, but My words will never pass away' (Matthew 24:35). Your truth is my foundation.

20. Lord, I declare that I am victorious in spiritual warfare, for

Your Word says, 'In all these things we are more than conquerors through Him who loved us' (Romans 8:37). I walk in authority and power.

**Closing Prayer:**
Father, I thank You for the authority to demolish every wicked thought and lie of the enemy. Renew my mind with Your truth, and fill my heart with peace and clarity. I stand firm in Your Word, knowing that victory is mine through Christ Jesus. In Jesus' name, Amen.

# CHAPTER 43

## Declarations Against Loneliness

*Scripture Focus:*
*"Never will I leave you; never will I forsake you."*
*Hebrews 13:5 (NIV)*

**Introduction:**
Loneliness is a deep and painful emotion that can leave one feeling isolated and forgotten. However, God's promise is sure: He will never leave nor forsake us. Hebrews 13:5 is a reminder that even in moments of solitude, God's presence is constant and His companionship is unwavering.

These declarations empower you to overcome feelings of loneliness by embracing the truth of God's presence and the fulfillment found in His love.

## 20 Declarations Against Loneliness

1. Father, in the name of Jesus, I decree and declare that I am never alone, for Your Word says, 'Never will I leave you; never will I forsake you' (Hebrews 13:5). Your presence surrounds me.

2. Lord, I declare that I am Your beloved, for Your Word says, 'I have loved you with an everlasting love; I have drawn you with unfailing kindness' (Jeremiah 31:3). I am deeply cherished by You.

3. I decree that I will not fear solitude, for Your Word says, 'Even though I walk through the darkest valley, I will fear no evil, for You are with me' (Psalm 23:4). Your rod and staff comfort me.

4. Father, I declare that I am complete in You, for Your Word says, 'In Christ you have been brought to fullness. He is the head over every power and authority' (Colossians 2:10). I lack nothing.

5. Lord, I decree that I will find joy in Your presence, for Your Word says, 'You make known to me the path of life; You will fill me with joy in Your presence' (Psalm 16:11). My heart overflows with joy.

6. I declare that I am surrounded by Your love, for Your Word says, 'For the mountains may depart and the hills be removed, but my steadfast love shall not depart from you' (Isaiah 54:10). Your love is eternal.

7. Father, I decree that I am upheld by Your hand, for Your Word says, 'Though he may stumble, he will not fall, for the Lord upholds him with His hand' (Psalm 37:24). I am sustained by You.

8. Lord, I declare that I will rest in Your peace, for Your Word says, 'And the peace of God, which transcends all understanding, will guard your hearts and your minds in Christ Jesus' (Philippians 4:7). Peace reigns in my heart.

9. I decree that I am never forgotten, for Your Word says, 'Can a mother forget the baby at her breast...? Though she may forget, I will not forget you!' (Isaiah 49:15). I am always on Your mind.

10. Father, I declare that I am hidden in You, for Your Word says, 'For you died, and your life is now hidden with Christ in God' (Colossians 3:3). I am secure in Your presence.

11. Lord, I decree that I will trust in Your companionship, for Your Word says, 'The Lord your God is with you, the Mighty Warrior who saves. He will take great delight in you' (Zephaniah 3:17). You rejoice over me.

12. I declare that my steps are ordered by You, for Your Word says, 'The steps of a good man are ordered by the Lord, and He delights in his way' (Psalm 37:23). You guide my every move.

13. Father, I decree that I will be content in every situation, for Your Word says, 'I have learned the secret of being content in any and every situation... I can do all this through Him who gives me strength' (Philippians 4:12-13). Contentment fills my heart.

14. Lord, I declare that I will not feel abandoned, for Your Word says, 'Though my father and mother forsake me, the Lord will receive me' (Psalm 27:10). You are my faithful Father.

15. I decree that I will walk in the joy of fellowship with You, for Your Word says, 'What we have seen and heard we proclaim also to you, so that you too may have fellowship with us; and indeed our fellowship is with the Father and with His Son Jesus Christ' (1 John 1:3). I am never isolated.

16. Father, I declare that You are my refuge, for Your Word says, 'God is our refuge and strength, an ever-present help in trouble' (Psalm 46:1). I find safety in You.

17. Lord, I decree that I will be surrounded by godly relationships, for Your Word says, 'A friend loves at all times, and a brother is born for a time of adversity' (Proverbs 17:17). You send the right people into my life.

18. I declare that I will focus on Your eternal promises, for Your Word says, 'And surely I am with you always, to the very end of the age' (Matthew 28:20). You are my eternal companion.

19. Father, I decree that I will walk in the hope of Your glory, for Your Word says, 'Christ in you, the hope of glory' (Colossians 1:27). I live with confident expectation.

20. Lord, I declare that I will not be shaken by loneliness, for Your Word says, 'Cast all your anxiety on Him because He cares for you' (1 Peter 5:7). I am cared for by You.

**Closing Prayer:**
Father, I thank You for Your abiding presence that casts out all loneliness. Help me to rest in Your promises and embrace the joy of Your companionship. Surround me with Your peace, and let my heart be filled with hope. In Jesus' name, Amen.

# SECTION 6

# OVERCOMING SPIRITUAL MANIPULATION

# CHAPTER 44

# Declarations to Break the Spirit of Rejection

**Scripture Focus:**
*"See, I have engraved you on the palms of My hands;
your walls are ever before Me."
Isaiah 49:16 (NIV)*

**Introduction:**
The spirit of rejection can lead to feelings of inadequacy, worthlessness, and abandonment. However, God's love is steadfast and unchanging. Isaiah 49:16 reminds us that we are engraved on His hands, a permanent mark of His care and affection. Breaking the spirit of rejection begins with embracing the truth of God's love and declaring His promises over your life.

These declarations will help you reject every lie of unworthiness and walk confidently in the acceptance and love of your Heavenly Father.

## 20 Declarations to Break the Spirit of Rejection

1. Father, in the name of Jesus, I decree and declare that I am fully accepted by You, for Your Word says, 'See, I have engraved you on the palms of My hands; your walls are ever before Me' (Isaiah 49:16). I am eternally loved.

2. Lord, I declare that I am chosen and not rejected, for Your Word says, 'You did not choose Me, but I chose you and appointed you so that you might go and bear fruit' (John 15:16). My identity is rooted in You.

3. I decree that every lie of rejection is silenced, for Your Word says, 'The thief comes only to steal and kill and destroy; I have come that they may have life, and have it to the full' (John 10:10). I choose Your abundant life.

4. Father, I declare that I am fearfully and wonderfully made, for Your Word says, 'I praise You because I am fearfully and wonderfully made; Your works are wonderful, I know that full well' (Psalm 139:14). I am a masterpiece of Your creation.

5. Lord, I decree that every root of rejection is uprooted, for Your Word says, 'Every plant that My heavenly Father has not planted will be pulled up by the roots' (Matthew 15:13). I am rooted in Your love.

6. I declare that I am a child of God, for Your Word says, 'See what great love the Father has lavished on us, that we should be called children of God!' (1 John 3:1). I belong to Your family.

7. Father, I decree that I am never alone, for Your Word says, 'Never will I leave you; never will I forsake you' (Hebrews 13:5). Your presence surrounds me.

8. Lord, I declare that my past does not define me, for Your Word says, 'Therefore, if anyone is in Christ, the new creation has come: The old has gone, the new is here!' (2 Corinthians 5:17). I am made new in You.

9. I decree that I am accepted and loved by You, for Your Word says, 'Accept one another, then, just as Christ accepted you, in order to bring praise to God' (Romans 15:7). I walk in Your acceptance.

10. Father, I declare that I am confident in Your love, for Your Word says, 'For I am convinced that neither death nor life, neither angels nor demons... nor anything else in all creation, will be able to separate us from the love of God' (Romans 8:38-39). I am inseparable from Your love.

11. Lord, I decree that I will not dwell on rejection, for Your Word says, 'Forget the former things; do not dwell on the past' (Isaiah 43:18). I focus on the new thing You are doing.

12. I declare that I am strong in You, for Your Word says, 'The Lord is my light and my salvation—whom shall I fear? The Lord is the stronghold of my life—of whom shall I be afraid?' (Psalm 27:1). I walk in boldness and strength.

13. Father, I decree that every chain of rejection is broken, for Your Word says, 'So if the Son sets you free, you will be free

indeed' (John 8:36). I live in complete freedom.

14. Lord, I declare that I am a part of Your Kingdom, for Your Word says, 'But you are a chosen people, a royal priesthood, a holy nation, God's special possession' (1 Peter 2:9). I am special in Your sight.

15. I decree that my identity is secure in You, for Your Word says, 'For we are God's handiwork, created in Christ Jesus to do good works, which God prepared in advance for us to do' (Ephesians 2:10). I am uniquely crafted for Your purpose.

16. Father, I declare that I am healed from emotional wounds, for Your Word says, 'He heals the brokenhearted and binds up their wounds' (Psalm 147:3). My heart is restored by Your love.

17. Lord, I decree that I will not fear rejection, for Your Word says, 'The Lord your God is with you, the Mighty Warrior who saves. He will take great delight in you; in His love He will no longer rebuke you, but will rejoice over you with singing' (Zephaniah 3:17). I rest in Your delight.

18. I declare that I will walk in the light of Your love, for Your Word says, 'The light shines in the darkness, and the darkness has not overcome it' (John 1:5). Darkness cannot prevail over me.

19. Father, I decree that every curse of rejection is canceled, for Your Word says, 'Christ redeemed us from the curse of the law by becoming a curse for us' (Galatians 3:13). I live under Your blessing.

20. Lord, I declare that I will embrace the fullness of Your love, for Your Word says, 'And so we know and rely on the love God has for us. God is love' (1 John 4:16). I rely on Your unfailing love.

**Closing Prayer:**
Father, I thank You for breaking the spirit of rejection over my life. I embrace Your everlasting love and the truth of my identity in You. Heal every wound caused by rejection, and let my heart overflow with Your peace and joy. In Jesus' name, Amen.

# CHAPTER 45

## Declarations Against Wet Dreams

**Scripture Focus:**
*"For the mind governed by the flesh is death, but the mind governed by the Spirit is life and peace."*
*Romans 8:6 (NIV)*

**Introduction:**
Wet dreams can be a result of subconscious thoughts influenced by spiritual or physical factors. They can leave individuals feeling condemned or spiritually attacked. Romans 8:6 highlights the importance of governing the mind through the Spirit, leading to life and peace. These declarations aim to address the root causes, cleanse the mind, and align every thought with God's Word and purity.

## 20 Declarations Against Wet Dreams

1. Father, in the name of Jesus, I decree and declare that my mind is governed by Your Spirit, for Your Word says, 'The mind governed by the Spirit is life and peace' (Romans 8:6). I reject every impurity.

2. Lord, I declare that I am free from every subconscious attack, for Your Word says, 'For though we live in the world, we do not wage war as the world does. The weapons we fight with have divine power to demolish strongholds' (2 Corinthians 10:3-4). Every stronghold is destroyed.

3. I decree that I take every thought captive to Christ, for Your Word says, 'We take captive every thought to make it obedient to Christ' (2 Corinthians 10:5). My thoughts align with Your truth.

4. Father, I declare that my dreams are sanctified, for Your Word says, 'He gives His beloved sleep' (Psalm 127:2). My rest is holy and protected.

5. Lord, I decree that every spirit of lust is uprooted, for Your Word says, 'Put to death, therefore, whatever belongs to your earthly nature: sexual immorality, impurity, lust, evil desires' (Colossians 3:5). I crucify the flesh.

6. I declare that my body is a temple of the Holy Spirit, for Your Word says, 'Do you not know that your bodies are temples of the Holy Spirit?' (1 Corinthians 6:19). My body is consecrated to You.

7. Father, I decree that every doorway to impure thoughts is

closed, for Your Word says, 'Do not give the devil a foothold' (Ephesians 4:27). I shut every access point to the enemy.

8. Lord, I declare that my mind is renewed, for Your Word says, 'Do not conform to the pattern of this world, but be transformed by the renewing of your mind' (Romans 12:2). My thoughts are purified by You.

9. I decree that every hidden sin is exposed and forgiven, for Your Word says, 'If we confess our sins, He is faithful and just to forgive us our sins and to purify us from all unrighteousness' (1 John 1:9). I am cleansed by Your blood.

10. Father, I declare that I will meditate on what is pure, for Your Word says, 'Whatever is true, whatever is noble, whatever is right, whatever is pure... think about such things' (Philippians 4:8). My mind dwells on purity.

11. Lord, I decree that every generational curse is broken, for Your Word says, 'Christ redeemed us from the curse of the law by becoming a curse for us' (Galatians 3:13). I am free from inherited patterns.

12. I declare that I walk in victory, for Your Word says, 'For the Lord your God is the One who goes with you to fight for you against your enemies to give you victory' (Deuteronomy 20:4). I am victorious in every battle.

13. Father, I decree that I am clothed in righteousness, for Your Word says, 'I delight greatly in the Lord; my soul rejoices in my God. For He has clothed me with garments of salvation' (Isaiah

61:10). I am covered by Your holiness.

14. Lord, I declare that my dreams will reflect Your peace, for Your Word says, 'You will keep in perfect peace those whose minds are steadfast, because they trust in You' (Isaiah 26:3). My rest is guarded by Your peace.

15. I decree that I resist every attack of the enemy, for Your Word says, 'Submit yourselves, then, to God. Resist the devil, and he will flee from you' (James 4:7). The enemy flees from me.

16. Father, I declare that every covenant with impurity is broken, for Your Word says, 'Make no covenant with them and show them no mercy' (Deuteronomy 7:2). I reject every unholy agreement.

17. Lord, I decree that my spirit is strengthened, for Your Word says, 'The Lord is faithful, and He will strengthen you and protect you from the evil one' (2 Thessalonians 3:3). I am fortified by Your power.

18. I declare that my thoughts are anointed by You, for Your Word says, 'But we have the mind of Christ' (1 Corinthians 2:16). I think with divine clarity.

19. Father, I decree that I will not entertain lustful imaginations, for Your Word says, 'I have made a covenant with my eyes; why then should I look upon a young woman?' (Job 31:1). My eyes and thoughts are holy.

20. Lord, I declare that every spirit influencing unclean dreams is

cast out, for Your Word says, 'In My name they will drive out demons' (Mark 16:17). I walk in deliverance and authority.

**Closing Prayer:**
Father, I thank You for breaking every influence over my dreams and subconscious mind. Purify my thoughts, sanctify my rest, and protect me from every attack of the enemy. Let my dreams reflect Your peace and glory. In Jesus' name, Amen.

# CHAPTER 46

# Declarations Against Breakup and Heartbreak

**Scripture Focus:**
*"He heals the brokenhearted and binds up their wounds."*
*Psalm 147:3 (NIV)*

**Introduction:**
Heartbreak and breakup can leave emotional scars, but God is near to the brokenhearted. Psalm 147:3 reassures us of His power to heal and restore. As you declare God's promises, His healing will mend your heart and bring peace, preparing you for the future He has planned.

## 20 Declarations Against Breakup and Heartbreak

1. Father, in the name of Jesus, I decree and declare that You heal my broken heart, for Your Word says, 'He heals the brokenhearted and binds up their wounds' (Psalm 147:3). My heart is restored.

2. Lord, I declare that You are close to me in my pain, for Your Word says, 'The Lord is close to the brokenhearted and saves those who are crushed in spirit' (Psalm 34:18). I am comforted by Your presence.

3. I decree that every wound caused by heartbreak is healed, for Your Word says, 'But I will restore you to health and heal your wounds, declares the Lord' (Jeremiah 30:17). My soul is whole.

4. Father, I declare that my future is secure, for Your Word says, 'For I know the plans I have for you, declares the Lord, plans to prosper you and not to harm you' (Jeremiah 29:11). I trust in Your purpose.

5. Lord, I decree that I will not dwell on the past, for Your Word says, 'Forget the former things; do not dwell on the past. See, I am doing a new thing!' (Isaiah 43:18-19). I focus on the new blessings You are bringing.

6. I declare that I am not defined by rejection, for Your Word says, 'You are a chosen people, a royal priesthood, a holy nation, God's special possession' (1 Peter 2:9). I am chosen and loved by You.

7. Father, I decree that I will walk in forgiveness, for Your Word says, 'Forgive as the Lord forgave you' (Colossians 3:13). I release every hurt and offense.

8. Lord, I declare that my heart is guarded, for Your Word says, 'Above all else, guard your heart, for everything you do flows from it' (Proverbs 4:23). I protect my emotions with Your wisdom.

9. I decree that You are my refuge, for Your Word says, 'God is our refuge and strength, an ever-present help in trouble' (Psalm 46:1). I find shelter in You.

10. Father, I declare that my tears are not wasted, for Your Word says, 'You keep track of all my sorrows. You have collected all my tears in Your bottle' (Psalm 56:8). You care for me deeply.

11. Lord, I decree that my heart will rejoice again, for Your Word says, 'Weeping may endure for a night, but joy comes in the morning' (Psalm 30:5). Joy is my portion.

12. I declare that I will not let bitterness take root, for Your Word says, 'See to it that no bitter root grows up to cause trouble and defile many' (Hebrews 12:15). I uproot every bitterness.

13. Father, I decree that my worth is in You, for Your Word says, 'For we are God's handiwork, created in Christ Jesus to do good works' (Ephesians 2:10). I am valuable in Your eyes.

14. Lord, I declare that You will replace my ashes with beauty, for Your Word says, 'To bestow on them a crown of beauty instead of

ashes, the oil of joy instead of mourning' (Isaiah 61:3). My life will reflect Your glory.

15. I decree that I will not fear the future, for Your Word says, 'Do not fear, for I am with you; do not be dismayed, for I am your God' (Isaiah 41:10). I trust in Your guidance.

16. Father, I declare that my heart will remain tender, for Your Word says, 'I will remove from you your heart of stone and give you a heart of flesh' (Ezekiel 36:26). I will love again with Your grace.

17. Lord, I decree that You will redeem this season, for Your Word says, 'And we know that in all things God works for the good of those who love Him' (Romans 8:28). This heartbreak will serve Your purpose.

18. I declare that I am victorious over emotional pain, for Your Word says, 'But thanks be to God! He gives us the victory through our Lord Jesus Christ' (1 Corinthians 15:57). I walk in victory.

19. Father, I decree that I will not be anxious, for Your Word says, 'Cast all your anxiety on Him because He cares for you' (1 Peter 5:7). I release every worry to You.

20. Lord, I declare that I am whole in You, for Your Word says, 'And the God of all grace... will Himself restore you and make you strong, firm, and steadfast' (1 Peter 5:10). My restoration is complete.

**Closing Prayer:**

Father, I thank You for healing my broken heart. I trust You to turn this season of pain into a testimony of Your faithfulness. Renew my joy, restore my hope, and prepare me for the blessings You have in store. In Jesus' name, Amen.

# CHAPTER 47

## Declarations Against Anxiety for the Future

***Scripture Focus:***
*"For I know the plans I have for you, declares the Lord, plans to prosper you and not to harm you, plans to give you hope and a future."*
*Jeremiah 29:11 (NIV)*

**Introduction:**
Anxiety about the future can rob you of peace and paralyze your faith. God has promised to prosper you and lead you into a hopeful future. Jeremiah 29:11 assures us of His good plans. These declarations will help you replace anxiety with trust and confidence in God's divine guidance.

## 20 Declarations Against Anxiety for the Future

1. Father, in the name of Jesus, I decree and declare that my future is secure in You, for Your Word says, 'For I know the plans I have for you... to give you hope and a future' (Jeremiah 29:11). I walk in Your plans.

2. Lord, I declare that I will not be anxious, for Your Word says, 'Do not be anxious about anything, but in every situation, by prayer and petition, with thanksgiving, present your requests to God' (Philippians 4:6). I choose prayer over worry.

3. I decree that Your peace guards my heart, for Your Word says, 'The peace of God... will guard your hearts and your minds in Christ Jesus' (Philippians 4:7). Peace reigns in me.

4. Father, I declare that I trust in You, for Your Word says, 'Trust in the Lord with all your heart and lean not on your own understanding' (Proverbs 3:5). My trust is unshakable.

5. Lord, I decree that I will not fear, for Your Word says, 'For God has not given us a spirit of fear, but of power and of love and of a sound mind' (2 Timothy 1:7). I walk in boldness.

6. I declare that You are my guide, for Your Word says, 'The Lord will guide you always; He will satisfy your needs in a sun-scorched land' (Isaiah 58:11). I am led by Your hand.

7. Father, I decree that every anxious thought is taken captive, for Your Word says, 'Take captive every thought to make it obedient to Christ' (2 Corinthians 10:5). My mind aligns with Your truth.

8. Lord, I declare that I will not fear the unknown, for Your Word says, 'Do not fear, for I am with you; do not be dismayed, for I am your God' (Isaiah 41:10). You are my assurance.

9. I decree that I will meditate on Your promises, for Your Word says, 'Keep this Book of the Law always on your lips; meditate on it day and night' (Joshua 1:8). Your Word is my anchor.

10. Father, I declare that I am confident in Your faithfulness, for Your Word says, 'The One who calls you is faithful, and He will do it' (1 Thessalonians 5:24). I rely on Your faithfulness.

11. Lord, I decree that my steps are ordered by You, for Your Word says, 'The steps of a good man are ordered by the Lord' (Psalm 37:23). I walk in divine alignment.

12. I declare that my future is filled with hope, for Your Word says, 'May the God of hope fill you with all joy and peace as you trust in Him' (Romans 15:13). Hope fills my heart.

13. Father, I decree that I will not be shaken by uncertainty, for Your Word says, 'I have set the Lord always before me; because He is at my right hand, I shall not be shaken' (Psalm 16:8). My faith is firm.

14. Lord, I declare that I will not be consumed by worry, for Your Word says, 'Cast all your anxiety on Him because He cares for you' (1 Peter 5:7). I release every worry to You.

15. I decree that my future is fruitful, for Your Word says, 'You will be like a well- watered garden, like a spring whose waters

never fail' (Isaiah 58:11). My life overflows with abundance.

16. Father, I declare that You make a way for me, for Your Word says, 'I will even make a way in the wilderness, and rivers in the desert' (Isaiah 43:19). I trust in Your provision.

17. Lord, I decree that my confidence is in You, for Your Word says, 'Being confident of this, that He who began a good work in you will carry it on to completion' (Philippians 1:6). You will finish what You started.

18. I declare that I will stand firm in faith, for Your Word says, 'Stand firm, and you will see the deliverance the Lord will bring you today' (Exodus 14:13). My faith is immovable.

19. Father, I decree that I walk in victory, for Your Word says, 'But thanks be to God! He gives us the victory through our Lord Jesus Christ' (1 Corinthians 15:57). I am victorious in Christ.

20. Lord, I declare that I embrace the future You have for me, for Your Word says, 'For the Lord your God is bringing you into a good land' (Deuteronomy 8:7). My future is blessed.

**Closing Prayer:**
Father, I thank You for replacing my anxiety with confidence in Your plan. Help me to trust in Your guidance and rest in Your peace. I look forward to the future with hope, knowing that You are leading me every step of the way. In Jesus' name, Amen.

# SECTION 7

# ESTABLISHING GENERATIONAL BLESSINGS

# Chapter 48

## Declarations Against Prophetic Manipulation

***Scripture Focus:***
*"Dear friends, do not believe every spirit, but test the spirits to see whether they are from God."*
*1 John 4:1 (NIV)*

**Introduction:**
Prophetic manipulation occurs when individuals misuse the gift of prophecy to control, deceive, or exploit others. God calls His children to discern truth from error and to rely on the guidance of the Holy Spirit. 1 John 4:1 reminds us to test every spirit to ensure it aligns with God's Word.

These declarations will strengthen your discernment, protect you from spiritual manipulation, and empower you to walk in the truth of God's Word.

## 20 Declarations Against Prophetic Manipulation

1. Father, in the name of Jesus, I decree and declare that I will test every spirit, for Your Word says, 'Dear friends, do not believe every spirit, but test the spirits to see whether they are from God' (1 John 4:1). I walk in discernment.

2. Lord, I declare that I will not be led astray, for Your Word says, 'See to it that no one takes you captive through hollow and deceptive philosophy' (Colossians 2:8). My mind is guarded by Your truth.

3. I decree that I will seek wisdom from You, for Your Word says, 'If any of you lacks wisdom, you should ask God, who gives generously to all without finding fault' (James 1:5). My decisions are guided by Your wisdom.

4. Father, I declare that I will not fear false prophets, for Your Word says, 'Beware of false prophets, who come to you in sheep's clothing, but inwardly are ravenous wolves' (Matthew 7:15). I am vigilant and protected.

5. Lord, I decree that I will rely on the Holy Spirit, for Your Word says, 'When He, the Spirit of truth, comes, He will guide you into all the truth' (John 16:13). Your Spirit leads me into truth.

6. I declare that every false word spoken over my life is nullified, for Your Word says, 'No weapon formed against you shall prosper, and every tongue which rises against you in judgment you shall condemn' (Isaiah 54:17). False words have no power over me.

7. Father, I decree that I will discern truth from error, for Your Word says, 'For God is not a God of confusion but of peace' (1 Corinthians 14:33). I walk in clarity and peace.

8. Lord, I declare that I will meditate on Your Word, for Your Word says, 'Your word is a lamp to my feet and a light to my path' (Psalm 119:105). Your Word illuminates my way.

9. I decree that I will not be deceived by flattery, for Your Word says, 'A flattering mouth works ruin' (Proverbs 26:28). I reject manipulative words.

10. Father, I declare that my heart will remain pure, for Your Word says, 'Blessed are the pure in heart, for they shall see God' (Matthew 5:8). I guard my heart against deception.

11. Lord, I decree that I will judge prophecy according to Your Word, for Your Word says, 'Do not quench the Spirit. Do not treat prophecies with contempt but test them all; hold on to what is good' (1 Thessalonians 5:19-21). I embrace what is true and reject what is false.

12. I declare that I will seek counsel from godly leaders, for Your Word says, 'Plans fail for lack of counsel, but with many advisers they succeed' (Proverbs 15:22). Wise counsel protects me.

13. Father, I decree that I will not be bound by fear, for Your Word says, 'For God gave us a spirit not of fear but of power and love and self-control' (2 Timothy 1:7). I walk boldly in Your truth.

14. Lord, I declare that I will test prophecy by its fruit, for Your

Word says, 'You will recognize them by their fruits' (Matthew 7:16). I discern by the fruit of the Spirit.

15. I decree that I will not be controlled by manipulation, for Your Word says, 'You were bought at a price; do not become slaves of human beings' (1 Corinthians 7:23). I belong to You alone.

16. Father, I declare that I will recognize deception, for Your Word says, 'For such people are false apostles, deceitful workers, masquerading as apostles of Christ' (2 Corinthians 11:13). I see through every disguise of the enemy.

17. Lord, I decree that I will walk in the light, for Your Word says, 'The light shines in the darkness, and the darkness has not overcome it' (John 1:5). I am protected by Your light.

18. I declare that I am anchored in Your Word, for Your Word says, 'Heaven and earth will pass away, but My words will never pass away' (Matthew 24:35). Your Word is my foundation.

19. Father, I decree that I will avoid the influence of false teachers, for Your Word says, 'They will secretly introduce destructive heresies' (2 Peter 2:1). I am shielded from heresy.

20. Lord, I declare that I will walk in the truth of Your promises, for Your Word says, 'And you will know the truth, and the truth will set you free' (John 8:32). I am free from every manipulation.

**Closing Prayer:**
Father, thank You for opening my eyes to discern truth from

error. Protect me from every form of prophetic manipulation, and lead me in the light of Your Word. Let my life be guided by Your Spirit and truth. In Jesus' name, Amen.

# CHAPTER 49

## Declarations Against Love Spells and Incantations

**Scripture Focus:**
*"There is no divination against Jacob, no evil omens against Israel. It will now be said of Jacob and of Israel, 'See what God has done!'"*
*Numbers 23:23 (NIV)*

**Introduction:**
The enemy seeks to manipulate hearts and derail destinies through love spells, enchantments, and incantations. Numbers 23:23 reassures believers that no divination or evil power can prevail against the children of God. These declarations will destroy every work of witchcraft and establish God's protection over your life and relationships.

## 20 Declarations Against Love Spells and Incantations

1. Father, in the name of Jesus, I decree and declare that no spell or incantation shall succeed against me, for Your Word says, 'There is no divination against Jacob, no evil omens against Israel' (Numbers 23:23). I stand in Your divine protection.

2. Lord, I declare that every work of witchcraft is nullified, for Your Word says, 'The Son of God appeared to destroy the devil's work' (1 John 3:8). Every evil scheme is destroyed.

3. I decree that no weapon formed against my relationships shall prosper, for Your Word says, 'No weapon forged against you will prevail' (Isaiah 54:17). My heart and relationships are secure.

4. Father, I declare that my destiny is untouchable, for Your Word says, 'The Lord will fight for you; you need only to be still' (Exodus 14:14). I rest in Your victory.

5. Lord, I decree that every enchantment and evil word spoken against me is canceled, for Your Word says, 'For the Lord your God is the one who goes with you to fight for you against your enemies to give you victory' (Deuteronomy 20:4).

6. I declare that I am covered by the blood of Jesus, for Your Word says, 'They triumphed over him by the blood of the Lamb and by the word of their testimony' (Revelation 12:11). The blood shields me from all evil.

7. Father, I decree that my life is hidden in You, for Your Word says, 'The name of the Lord is a fortified tower; the righteous run

to it and are safe' (Proverbs 18:10). I am secure in Your name.

8. Lord, I declare that every plan of the enemy is exposed and defeated, for Your Word says, 'Nothing in all creation is hidden from God's sight' (Hebrews 4:13). I walk in Your light.

9. I decree that every chain of manipulation is broken, for Your Word says, 'So if the Son sets you free, you will be free indeed' (John 8:36). I am free from all control.

10. Father, I declare that I walk in Your authority, for Your Word says, 'I have given you authority to trample on snakes and scorpions and to overcome all the power of the enemy' (Luke 10:19). I exercise dominion.

11. Lord, I decree that my relationships are aligned with Your will, for Your Word says, 'Trust in the Lord with all your heart and lean not on your own understanding' (Proverbs 3:5). I trust Your plans for my heart.

12. I declare that I am guarded by Your angels, for Your Word says, 'For He will command His angels concerning you to guard you in all your ways' (Psalm 91:11). I am divinely protected.

13. Father, I decree that every spell is powerless, for Your Word says, 'Resist the devil, and he will flee from you' (James 4:7). The enemy has no hold over me.

14. Lord, I declare that I will not fear any evil, for Your Word says, 'Even though I walk through the darkest valley, I will fear no evil, for You are with me' (Psalm 23:4). You are my protector.

15. I decree that my heart is consecrated to You, for Your Word says, 'Above all else, guard your heart, for everything you do flows from it' (Proverbs 4:23). I guard my emotions with Your wisdom.

16. Father, I declare that all darkness is banished, for Your Word says, 'The light shines in the darkness, and the darkness has not overcome it' (John 1:5). Light prevails in my life.

17. Lord, I decree that Your truth dismantles every deception, for Your Word says, 'You will know the truth, and the truth will set you free' (John 8:32). I walk in liberty.

18. I declare that every attempt to derail my relationships is futile, for Your Word says, 'The Lord foils the plans of the nations; He thwarts the purposes of the peoples' (Psalm 33:10). Your purpose stands firm.

19. Father, I decree that I will discern every false word, for Your Word says, 'Do not believe every spirit, but test the spirits to see whether they are from God' (1 John 4:1). I walk in discernment.

20. Lord, I declare that my love life is consecrated to You, for Your Word says, 'Love must be sincere. Hate what is evil; cling to what is good' (Romans 12:9). I honor You in my relationships.

**Closing Prayer:**
Father, I thank You for breaking every spell, incantation, and plan of the enemy over my life. I declare that my heart, emotions, and relationships are under Your divine authority. Let Your truth, love, and light prevail in all areas of my life. In Jesus' name, Amen.

# Declarations Against Fear of Making the Wrong Choice

**Scripture Focus:**
*"Whether you turn to the right or to the left, your ears will hear a voice behind you, saying, 'This is the way; walk in it.'"*
*Isaiah 30:21 (NIV)*

**Introduction:**
Fear of making the wrong choice can lead to indecision and anxiety. Isaiah 30:21 reminds us that God provides guidance and clarity when we seek Him. These declarations will help you overcome fear, trust in God's wisdom, and confidently make decisions aligned with His will.

## 20 Declarations Against Fear of Making the Wrong Choice

1. Father, in the name of Jesus, I decree and declare that You guide my steps, for Your Word says, 'Whether you turn to the right or to the left, your ears will hear a voice behind you, saying, "This is the way; walk in it"' (Isaiah 30:21). I trust Your direction.

2. Lord, I declare that I will not fear, for Your Word says, 'For I know the plans I have for you... plans to give you hope and a future' (Jeremiah 29:11). Your plans are good.

3. I decree that I will not be anxious about decisions, for Your Word says, 'Do not be anxious about anything, but in every situation... present your requests to God' (Philippians 4:6). I rest in Your peace.

4. Father, in the name of Jesus, I decree and declare that You guide my steps, for Your Word says, 'Whether you turn to the right or to the left, your ears will hear a voice behind you, saying, "This is the way; walk in it"' (Isaiah 30:21). I trust Your direction.

5. Lord, I declare that I will not fear, for Your Word says, 'For I know the plans I have for you... plans to give you hope and a future' (Jeremiah 29:11). Your plans are good.

6. I decree that I will not be anxious about decisions, for Your Word says, 'Do not be anxious about anything, but in every situation... present your requests to God' (Philippians 4:6). I rest in Your peace.

7. Father, I decree that I will walk in the light of Your Word, for Your Word says, 'Your word is a lamp to my feet and a light to my path' (Psalm 119:105). My steps are illuminated by Your truth.

8. Lord, I declare that every decision I make will align with Your will, for Your Word says, 'Do not conform to the pattern of this world, but be transformed by the renewing of your mind. Then you will be able to test and approve what God's will is
—His good, pleasing, and perfect will' (Romans 12:2). My mind is renewed by Your Spirit.

9. I decree that I will seek Your counsel, for Your Word says, 'Blessed is the one who does not walk in step with the wicked or stand in the way that sinners take or sit in the company of mockers' (Psalm 1:1). I follow the path of righteousness.

10. Father, I declare that You will establish my steps, for Your Word says, 'The steps of a good man are ordered by the Lord, and He delights in His way' (Psalm 37:23). My path is secure in You.

11. Lord, I decree that I will not fear failure, for Your Word says, 'For the righteous falls seven times and rises again' (Proverbs 24:16). I rise in Your strength.

12. I declare that my heart is at peace, for Your Word says, 'Let the peace of Christ rule in your hearts, since as members of one body you were called to peace' (Colossians 3:15). I am ruled by Your peace.

13. Father, I decree that my decisions are guided by wisdom, for Your Word says, 'If any of you lacks wisdom, you should ask God,

who gives generously to all without finding fault, and it will be given to you' (James 1:5). I am filled with divine wisdom.

14. Lord, I declare that I will trust the outcome to You, for Your Word says, 'Commit to the Lord whatever you do, and He will establish your plans' (Proverbs 16:3). My efforts are blessed by Your hands.

15. I decree that I will not be influenced by fear, for Your Word says, 'For God has not given us a spirit of fear, but of power and of love and of a sound mind' (2 Timothy 1:7). I walk in power and clarity.

16. Father, I declare that I will walk in understanding, for Your Word says, 'The unfolding of Your words gives light; it gives understanding to the simple' (Psalm 119:130). Your wisdom enlightens me.

17. Lord, I decree that my decisions will bear good fruit, for Your Word says, 'You will recognize them by their fruits' (Matthew 7:16). My life will produce the fruit of righteousness.

18. I declare that I will not rush into decisions, for Your Word says, 'Whoever is patient has great understanding, but one who is quick-tempered displays folly' (Proverbs 14:29). I wait on Your timing.

19. Father, I decree that I will rely on Your Spirit, for Your Word says, 'Not by might nor by power, but by My Spirit,' says the Lord Almighty' (Zechariah 4:6). I am led by Your Spirit.

20. Lord, I declare that I will trust You with all my heart, for Your Word says, 'Be still, and know that I am God; I will be exalted among the nations' (Psalm 46:10). I rest in Your sovereignty.

**Closing Prayer:**

Father, thank You for silencing every fear and aligning my heart with Your will. Lead me in Your wisdom and let my decisions glorify You. May I walk in faith, trusting that Your plans for me are good. In Jesus' name, Amen.

# OTHER TITLES BY TOMI ARAYOMI

This bold manifesto challenges believers to rise and become the devil's worst nightmare. Tomi Arayomi outlines how to take dominion in culture, business, and daily life by walking in apostolic authority.

A raw and honest examination of the cultural Christianity that dilutes biblical truth. Tomi Arayomi confronts the spirit of compromise that dresses like a sheep but devours like a wolf. This book calls believers to shed cultural conformity and return to authentic faith.

This energizing book explores the prophetic lifestyle as a rhythm, not a moment. Tomi Arayomi shares practical wisdom and supernatural insights for those called to hear and speak the voice of God. It's a fun, relatable, and equipping guide to living prophetically in everyday life.

In this book, Tomi Arayomi unlocks spiritual secrets hidden in plain sight; truths Jesus reserved for the mature. It's for believers ready to handle revelation that transforms how we see the Kingdom.

This book is a prophetic guide to engaging in the first fruits fast, a biblical principle for acceleration and divine momentum. It is a powerful tool for those seeking divine recovery, clarity, and supernatural breakthrough.

A strategic prayer guide for singles who desire a godly spouse and wholeness before marriage. It's more than a prayer book—it's a preparation manual.

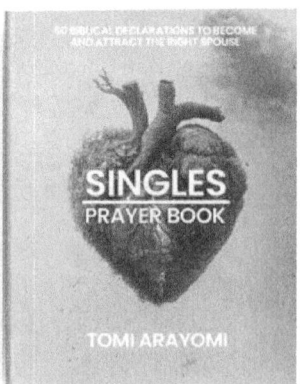

This powerful book offers 50 declarations to protect, heal, and strengthen your marriage. A must-have tool for every married believer who desires to Satan-proof their covenant.

A no-nonsense prayer manual against witchcraft, voodoo, Santería, and occultic altars. Tomi Arayomi exposes the strategies of darkness and provides 50 targeted prayers for deliverance and freedom.

A revelatory expose uncovering the 10 spiritual gates through which hell attempts to infiltrate believers' lives. This is a clarion call to take back spiritual territory and walk in uncompromised authority.

**Connect with Tomi Arayomi**

Thank you for reading and praying through this book. We would love to hear how these declarations have blessed your personal life. Stay connected with us on social media and visit our website for more resources and updates:

- Website: [www.TomiArayomi.com](www.TomiArayomi.com)
- Instagram: @TomiArayomi
- Facebook: @Tomi Arayomi
- YouTube: @Tomi Arayomi

Join Command Your Morning
Start your day in prophetic prayer with Tomi Arayomi
**Live every Monday to Friday at 5:00 AM CST**
Watch on: youtube.com/CommandYourMorningTomiArayomi

Scan to join Telegram Group:

Printed in Dunstable, United Kingdom

66048870R00151